THE CENTURY SPEAKS

THE CENTURY SPEAKS

Recollections of Lancashire
over the last 100 years

Phil Smith

Carnegie Publishing Ltd

First published in 1999 by
Carnegie Publishing Ltd,
Carnegie House,
Chatsworth Road,
Lancaster LA1 4SL

Copyright © BBC Radio Lancashire 1999

British Library Cataloguing-in-Publication data
A catalogue record for this book is available from the British Library

ISBN 1-85936-069-6

Typeset and originated by Carnegie Publishing Ltd
Printed and bound by Redwood Books, Trowbridge

All old photographs by kind permission of
Lancashire County Libraries (East Lancashire Division)

Modern photographs taken by Ian Lewis,
except for that on page 44 which is by kind permission of
the *Lancashire Evening Post*

Dedicated to the memory of
Ron Carter, blacksmith

Contents

The odd amputated chimney left.

Introduction

$\mathcal{P}$ROGRESS has never obliterated the past quite like it has done over the last fifty years. When I look around the old milltowns of North-East Lancashire, searching for the familiar things I knew as a child, I might be in another world from the one I was raised in. The mill chimneys which loomed over us – like totems to the Great God Cotton – have all but disappeared. The odd, amputated thing, sprouting weeds and a haphazard home to a roosting kestrel, pokes up apologetically.

The air that once hung heavy with coal smoke seems breathtakingly clear, our ancient hill stepping ever closer. Perhaps a saw-toothed roof of a weaving shed still remains, the stonework stained with rust where the troughings are leaking, or maybe the old keep of an engine house. But plans are in the pipeline ... another superstore, another leisure centre ...

That building on the hill, the one that gapes like an old, black tooth, could it have been a Methodist chapel? Even our terraced houses have changed in the wake of stone cleaning and the Dulux revolution; whole rows plucked away, leaving light, air and greenery. You need to play detective to unearth even the recent past. Was the grand shop front with the stone carbels once the old Co-op (it's now the chapel of rest)? And scattered amongst the breezeblock and plastic façades of today's take-aways and video shops shine the real stonework legacies. Sandstone architecture that glows with the subtle warmth of dry sherry, a dulled plaque celebrating the generosity of a long-forgotten alderman – a hidden statue that only the pigeons pay homage to.

But these ghosts of our past are sent shrinking into the shadows by modern life: the unrelenting traffic, the colourful onslaught of shoppers in their chain-store fashions, their football shirts and the baseball caps, their mobile phones and their well-filled bellies. Are these people really the grandchildren of the drab Lowryesque figures who traipsed, clog-footed, to the mills in a painful routine of hard-graft and monotony? Are the folk who witnessed their looms being smuggled through the mill's backdoor to

A new use for an old co-op.

'Edge closer and you will hear stories of those mills.'

some far-flung corner of the great British Empire really the same ones who stand, decades later, bronzed by the Mediterranean sun and chatting amiably at the bank? Yes, they are.

And if you stop by the big house, that was once the home of a millowner but is now a rest home, you can see the old people who have been wheeled out into the sun, their wrinkled, work-worn hands folded across their knees. You can almost see the century's memories flit across their blue-again eyes, and you know that the past lives on. For here lie memories that no stone paint or bulldozer can erase. If you edge closer and start to listen you will hear stories of those mills which filled our narrow valleys and whose looms echoed as far as the moor-tops. You will hear about life in those congested terraces where one tin bath served a whole street and one bed slept four children. You will learn of Whit walks under proud banners, trips into the countryside 'hedging and dyking', otter-watching in a favourite trout stream or helping in the hayfields on parched summer's evenings, then leaving the meadow and drinking with horses in the cattle trough.

Although the past may be obscured by the pell-mell progress of the present, it also lives on in the memories of the elderly. This is what this book is about. For six months, from the winter of 1998 to the spring of 1999, I interviewed and recorded over one hundred local people. Not all were old, but all had memories; all were able to offer their own insights into the astonishing changes that have made this century so different from any other. The information was harvested as part of a nationwide project by the BBC to celebrate the birth of a new millennium. Every local radio station in the country was involved, each producing a series for its own station, mine of course being BBC Radio Lancashire.

One day last October we all shuffled into a conference suite at Birmingham's Pebble Mill to report to the BBC grandees behind the project. Months before, with typical Birtian thoroughness, they had commissioned a hefty guide book outlining the themes for each programme, with introductions from sociologists and historians. They'd even listed possible questions they thought we might ask. Another part of the plan was to make the hours of interview material available to the British Library for historians and scholars of the future to have an oral record of how ordinary people felt and thought in the twentieth century.

It is reported that some of the interviewers sat in front of their subjects with their guide books open and painstakingly went through every question, clearly hopeful of later promotion. I'm ashamed to admit that I slung mine in a drawer and promptly forgot about it. Sociologists may be jolly good at telling us all what we already know about how many people watch soaps

History still lives in the memories of the elderly residents of an old people's home in Colne.

or eat TV dinners, but can they be trusted to make interesting radio programmes? Stories, not statistics, make good radio. Tales like those of Lizzie Hartley, born ninety-four years ago with an extra finger on each hand which the doctor snipped off and wanted to throw in the fire. But Lizzie's parents insisted that they be buried in a box in Colne cemetery with the body of her grandmother. Or Ben Barnes of Stacksteads trying to prise a coach-load of drunken day-trippers out of the pub and ending up having to dispose of an intoxicated, on-duty policeman! Or Alice Whittle of Leyland who took the advice of her grandmother and never went out with a boy without a safety pin in her knickers. Or why John Parkinson's canal barge became known as 'The Bodysnatcher'.

I've learnt about being blown up by an exploding steam engine; what it's like to drive a Royal Scot down Shap; how to kill a pig and make black puddings, or wrestle a steer at a rodeo in Nelson, or survive the Blitz; how to lose your false teeth in a swell in Morecambe Bay, or get arrested for playing pitch-and-toss for money in a potato field and marry a man who slept in his string vest ... and much, much more. All the tragic, sad, silly and wonderful stories that Lancashire people are famous for sharing with anyone within moments of meeting them.

However, interviewing isn't all an easy ride. Before you begin you must throw a blanket over the budgie's cage and convince him it's bed time. You have to learn how to dissuade the dog from jumping into your lap and slavering down your microphone without upsetting the owner. You have to stop 'her-from-next-door' from coming round to find out what's going on. And you must develop a liking for large quantities of Ginger Nuts and gallons of strong tea. After that, it's plain sailing.

For these are ordinary people like you and me. They are the unsung heroes of the everyday skirmishes and struggles of life, not the so-called experts or spokespersons for the human race so beloved of the media today. And although we might not be at the hub of things up here in Lancashire, that does not mean our views of life are any less lucid and sharp. Sometimes, I think we are like people living on the edge of a vast lake. We may miss the great upheavals of history and events on the world stage, but in time we catch the ripples and our responses are no less interesting and insightful than those who play a more central role. Take the Colne engine driver who recalls bringing his locomotive into Euston in 1947 at the time of Indian independence. On the platform he saw the returning civil servants with their expensive luggage and small army of servants, and watched the Rolls Royces whisking them off to early retirement in the leafy shires of southern England. The picture he paints says something new about the inequalities of the Empire; as he observes, 'I'd heard a lot about unemployment but this lot didn't look like they'd just been made unemployed'.

What follows are not simply radio transcripts. The radio series used a montage format, using the voices of those interviewed. This book is an attempt to comment upon the material of the programmes. And other stories and experiences which could not be included in the programmes due to time limitations can be found throughout these pages.

My opinions are my own, but if you find inaccuracies and things that do not accord with your own memories, then please bear in mind that I am reporting what other people have told me. I write not as an historian, nor as a sociologist (despite my BBC briefing!), but as someone who has spent the majority of his working life wandering around the region with a tape-recorder and listening to the voices of ordinary people. I hope the final product not only entertains but also casts light on this extraordinary century of change.

I should like to thank all the people I interviewed who gave so freely and generously of their time and experience, Ian Cook and my son, Elliot, for their editing of the radio programmes, Steve Taylor of Radio Lancashire, the staff of Lancashire County Library (East Lancashire Division), and all of those who have worked to produce this book before the end of the radio series.

Phil Smith
October 1999.

'The soot came down just as rain comes down today.'

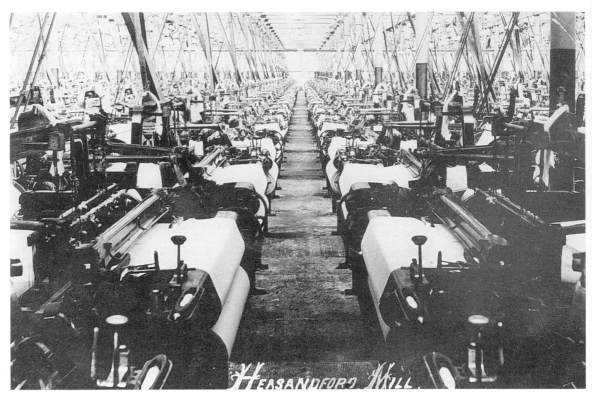

'Aisles between the looms disappearing into the distance.'

Chapter One

Where We Live

TITUS THORNBER'S description of Burnley after the First World War could have come straight out of the pages of Dickens' *Hard Times*. Titus was a schoolboy in the 1920s and for him his home town was a 'hell hole'.

'It was cotton everywhere. You'd only to walk through the street and there was cotton waste hanging from the telegraph wires. And the smell of cotton-seed oil everywhere, plus the smell of the coal-fired steam engines. The soot came down just as rain comes down today, so that there was dirt and blackness everywhere. You'd to get washed several times a day. Your neck was black, your knees were black, your hands and arms were black because everything you touched was covered in soot. Burnley and Wigan were music-hall jokes. The dirtiest and filthiest places on God's earth.'

Titus was the son of a textile manufacturer so had regular access to the inside of a cotton mill. Here the scene sounds to have come straight out of Pandemonium:

'In the background there was always the subdued roar of the weaving

Titus Thornber.

Could they have got the houses any closer to the mill? Burnley 1923.

sheds. But if you went inside, every time the swing doors opened a wave of sound came out and hit you like a battering ram. A mass of whirring machinery, belts and picking sticks lashing backwards and forwards. And great aisles between the looms disappearing into the distance. And gradually you realised that working amongst these were the women weavers. How they escaped being killed standing there in the middle of all this whirring machinery I'll never know.'

How many times do you have to multiply these scenes of external filth and internal chaos to get a picture of the whole of milltown Lancashire? But that it should all have disappeared so comprehensively within a generation is surely the most remarkable change the century has brought us. No one I've spoken to now in their mid-fifties or older wasn't in some way touched by this phenomenon of cotton. It is as if the fall-out from the mill chimneys is ingrained within our very souls.

You certainly couldn't get away from the soot in Burnley before the late 1950s. 'By 9 o'clock in the morning all the sparkle and brightness of the early sunshine went and you could see the smog rising from the valley and covering everything,' recalls Ken Spencer. And Lynn Millard remembers that the only time you could see the town from the surrounding heights was between late Saturday afternoon and Sunday teatime. This was the time when all the mill fires were damped down after the mills closed at Saturday dinner-time. But it was a short respite and the firebeaters were back in around 3.30 on Sunday afternoon to stoke the fires ready for another week of dirt and noise. 'And wealth, as well,' we are reminded by Titus Thornber. 'It might have been a sub-zero place but it was a necessary one because of the wealth it created.'

But while many of the recipients of that wealth were probably laughing at us in the music halls of London and the South, a price was being paid here in the milltowns of Lancashire. Albert Morris of Nelson recalls the acrid smell of sulphur that caught the back of his throat when it was smoggy. At times like that he was advised by his parents to put his hankie in front of his nose to breathe and he remembers how black it was when he removed it. TB and other respiratory diseases were rife. 'The whole town was terribly depressing,' says Lynn Millard. 'Burnley was said to have the highest suicide rate in the country in the 1930s.'

Titus Thornber observed three classes of housing in Burnley when he was young in the 1920s. There were the ones where he was fortunate enough to live, above the tidemark of smog on the outskirts of the town. These were where the millowners and managers lived. But then, to get down into town he would have to pass through a second area of well-built terraced

In the shadow of the mill. Note the donkeystoned steps even in this dank-looking back street.

houses with scrubbed fronts and washed paint-work, tributes to the house-wife's efforts at keeping the descending filth under control. These were the homes of the weavers. Then, descending even further to get into the town centre he had to pass through 'fearful slum areas, dreadful to walk through.' Here's how he describes them:

'They were horrible back-to-back houses thrown up at the beginning of the cotton era. When you looked in through the doors the poverty was appalling. Probably let for a shilling a week, the poorest people lived in them. First there were cellar dwellings, then one above, and paying a bit more to live above that. But the worst thing was getting rid of human excrement. They had no proper sewers and they emptied their chamber pots into the street gutters. You'd to be careful walking past because people used to empty them from the upstairs windows. It wasn't so bad if there was plenty of wet weather to keep the gutters flowing, but in warm, hot summer weather it became appalling. And children, dressed in rags, used to play marbles in the gutters.'

In the town centres a really bad smog would bring almost everything to a standstill. Stanley Graham remembers the smogs in Stockport, where he was brought up, being so full of sulphur that they were yellow. 'After dark, with only the streetlights on, you literally couldn't see your hand in front of your face. The only thing that kept you going were the trams.' He recalls the conductor walking in front with a smudge-pot, a cast-iron kettle with a spout into which a piece of rope was pushed and filled with waste oil. It gave out a flickering yellow light which showed up well in fog.

But at the busiest of times the town centres must have seemed every bit as noisy and chaotic as the mills themselves. We think with modern traffic we have a monopoly on noise pollution. But Albert Norris recalls a milltown main street full of the clatter of clogs, the clip-clop of horses and carts and the rending of metal against metal as the tramcars ground round the corners. I can find no record of whether the word stress meant anything to the people who had to live in such an environment.

One of the least enviable roles must have been that of the womenfolk. Twenty years ago I can remember interviewing one old man from Colne. It was about the time when keep-fit classes were becoming popular and a lady had been telling him what a good idea they were. 'Keep-fit classes?' he retorted sardonically, 'They had them 70 years ago when I was a little lad; keep-fit classes for women. They lasted all week. You should have seen th' arms they had on 'em in those days: wringing machines on Monday, one o' them great big things wi wooden rollers. Possers ...' And he listed the week's domestic drudgery, including a full-time job at the mill. 'There were not so many tranquillisers in those days. They were glad to get upstairs to bed. They had a hard life in those days.'

The women fought an endless battle against the dirt. Muriel Blenkinsop who lived in Bolton remembers the washday regime when she was a little girl.

'Washing day was a Monday and no coalman dare go up the back dad on that day. People also 'sweeled' their chimneys. This involved setting fire to the chimney to burn away the soot in order to save on a chimney-sweep. If anybody sweeled on a Monday they were not the flavour of the month because all the bits would fall down on the washing. We had a boiler in the cellar – they call it a set pan in Yorkshire – and mother was in the cellar all of Monday and it was all steam down there. And she'd be drying if she could in the back street, otherwise, when I came home from school

'Lonely sentinels of the industrial revolution'. The impressively restored 220 ft mill chimney at Ellenroad, near Rochdale.

in November on a cold night, there'd be the maiden round the fire and the clothes-rack above that, all full of drying clothes.'

At 94 Lizzie Hartley is still proud of how clean her flags are at the back of her terraced house in Colne. She recalls how spotlessly clean people kept the outsides of their houses in the old days. Mopping the steps and scouring them was a ritual every Saturday or Friday night. It had to be done. 'You never see anyone with a brush these days,' she complains. 'There's only us that swills out on this back dad.' But why bother, I want to know, with the incomprehension of a feckless son of the age of convenience and labour-saving devices.

'I like it!' cries Lizzie with a challenging glint in her blue eyes. 'It suits my ego to think that it's been done and it's clean. That's the way I look at it. My flags are the cleanest in the row on here.' And then she adds with a wistful note, 'Ay, let me have the old days back. They were wonderful.'

Nostalgia is, of course, a recurrent sentiment of a series like this. But it's a hankering after the values of the past rather than the material conditions. But Stanley Graham has a genuine admiration for the mill chimneys that did so much to turn the milltown of pre-war Lancashire into a hell hole. In the 1980s Stanley led a team which renovated the 220 foot chimney as part of a project to restore the giant steam engine at Ellenroad mill near Rochdale. To him the mill chimney is a statement of the millowner's self-image. 'If you're the wealthiest bloke in the area employing most people, you put up a chimney that says so.' It explains the fashion for ornate tops like the India Mill at Darwen or Manningham Mills in Bradford. Round Burnley the chimneys were plain, which perhaps reflects the down-to-earth no-nonsense approach we still prize as a northern virtue. Stanley is at pains to point out that the truncated specimens we see today are the result of the tops being taken off because of weathering to the unprotected brick-work. We no longer see them as they once were and to him they're 'spoilt'. But it's a heady world, the world of the chimney lover. One of Stanley's friends now owns 14 chimneys which he carefully looks after. He calls them 'the lonely sentinels of the Industrial Revolution' and he preserves them so that the rest of us can see them on the skyline and remember where we came from. To which I'd add: they're also monuments to an heroic army of workers who had to endure conditions that would make any modern Environmental Health officer blanch and hang up his clip-board.

Even in the surrounding Pennine countryside the effects of the smoke pollution were noticed. To this day you can escape the modern clamour of the town onto the moortops to find drystone walls still blackened with the fallout of soot from the old mills. Trevor Rushton, who farmed land above Burnley after the Second World War, could see the constant pall of smoke rising from the valleys so that even the hills were sometimes invisible. All the farm buildings and walls were black. Lichen, such a welcome feature of our gritstone walls today, simply didn't grow at all and there was hardly any moss. The pollution created such acid conditions in the soil that plant growth was retarded. And to add to Trevor's problems, the smoke increased the cloud cover that is such a constant feature of the Pennine sky. Titus Thornber remembers the effect of the soot on the sheep. When he went away from the area he found that sheep were white. 'They were a different species in Burnley. In Burnley the sheep were black and the dogs were black!'

In Wiswell, the village near Whalley, 95-year-old Florrie Birtwell remembers a time when everything was black at night. When she was a child there were no streetlamps in the village and no gas or electricity. Everything had to be done by oil lamp and she remembers watching her mother trimming the wicks. She enjoyed walking home in the dark, linking arms with her friends, singing old war songs like 'It's a long way to Tipperary' and 'Take me back to dear old Blighty.' During the Second World War David Palmer remembers the black-out in Barnoldswick. As a child he recalls the black-out man coming to check that all their blinds were drawn. The same man was the knocker-up as well as the town lamp-lighter. Sometimes while he lit his pipe and sat down and had a rest he would invite the kids to light some of the streetlamps.

'He used a pole with a flame on the end. We had to use the pole to push the glass of the lamp down and pull a chain to switch on the gas. "And don't touch t' mantle whatever tha does!" There was the devil to pay if the flimsy mantle got broken. At home we never seemed to have a mantle; ours was always a flame. People used to come running and knocking on the door shouting, "Mrs Palmer, Mrs Palmer, you've a fire in your kitchen!" But it was because we never had a mantle. It was useless because there were six kids and we all had plenty of friends and the door was forever opening and closing and if there was a mantle in it soon got broken. As soon as the door slammed my mother would cry, "That's my mantle again!" And there wouldn't be another one for weeks.'

During the 1950s Margaret McLean delivered newspapers in Burnley and remembers some very poor houses with no electricity. One was an old pub that had been converted into flats. Because no one was prepared to pay for any gaslight in the hallway, she remembers being absolutely terrified as a child groping her way inside in the pitch dark.

The knocker-up.

An idyllic escape
– one of the
many cloughs on
the fringes of the
mill towns.

Belching sulphurous chimneys, gutters running with sewage, roaring weaving sheds and noisy congested streets with dirt and blackness every-where, it's no wonder that people took their chance to escape into the countryside whenever they could. And because urban life sounds to have been so hellish, by contrast the countryside and the simplicity of the pleasures that it brought take on an idyllic quality which seems lost forever today.

Donald Barker who was born in the village of Water in Rossendale just before the First World War remembers escaping up onto the cloughs that run down into the valleys off the moors. He recalls one particular pool where he used to sit 'meditating'. The water was crystal clear where it ran through the sandstone rock and he used to watch insects and voles and other creatures. The rivers were full of trout, even the Irwell and the Whitewell. And then he'd climb up to watch the peewits wheeling on

Deerplay Moor. As children they'd sometimes make nets and put them over rabbit holes and shout down another hole in the vain expectation that the rabbits would come out and give themselves up.

There was an innocence about these rustic pursuits which makes hearing them all the more enchanting to a modern listener spoilt by too much over-sophistication. You catch a tone of wistfulness in the voices of the story-tellers which underlines the profound pleasure they must have felt with these simple pleasures. Nowhere more so than in the quiet, measured delivery of Edgar Wormwell. He takes us back to a pre-lapsarian world before we'd invented agro-chemicals and species were endangered. He remembers the rasping note of the corncrake in the church meadow, the ripple of skylarks, otters in the stream in the middle of the village of Kelbrook near Earby, and dragonflies 'six inch long and all colours'. He was another one who ventured up the cloughs onto the high moors, but not alone. 'In the 1930s when times were hard whole families used to go up there and they'd be there all summer.' He remembers watching dippers, Jenny Whitethroats, diving under the water to feed their young in the hidden roots of a tree. And the consternation of the mill manager when they dammed the beck that fed his mill lodge lower down, and John Willie would march up and half drown himself releasing the water. But as soon as his back was turned they'd dam it up again.

Almost unwittingly people became accomplished naturalists. Names of flowers and birds, trees and even grasses, were part of a common fund of knowledge possessed by people with access to the countryside. I can't help feeling that it was always like this and we are witnessing the end of a line that stretched back to a time when we all had our roots in the natural world before the Industrial Revolution chained us to time clocks and machinery and dreary urban terraces. There's a continuity that goes back thousands of years in which man lived and survived from his knowledge and understanding of nature. But the second half of the twentieth century has finally seen these links broken and to our shame today many of our children can't tell an oak from a sycamore or a lapwing from a curlew.

Schools helped to foster an interest in nature. At the village school in Wiswell Florrie Birtwell remembers winning thre'pence for being able to identify wild flowers she'd brought in. The hedgerows, she recalls, were full of primroses and wild strawberries. And Albert Morris used to enter wild fruits, hazelnuts, sycamore propellers, blackberries and bilberries in the children's classes at Barrowford show. He remembers winning prizes for wild grasses he'd collected, all graded and identified and placed in bottles on the trestle tables in the show tents.

The Spencer family haymaking, Wycoller, 1920.

Before motorcars and trips to Camelot, families used to go for walks together in the countryside. Retired farmer Trevor Rushton says the foot-paths across his land were so well worn that people didn't have to ask where they were. A popular time for a family walk would be after church on Sunday or at holiday time. Today such paths are barely used and you would be hard-pressed to find them. People prefer to jump into their cars and go to recognised beauty spots with lots of amenities like the Lake District or the National Parks.

One of the most fondly recalled occasions when the millworkers got a chance to refresh their ancient rural roots was haymaking time. Many families joined in and helped with the handwork: opening and shaking the hay from the swathes and loading the carts to bring the hay into the barns. Trevor Rushton recalls a regular seasonal pattern:

'In the smaller cotton villages, communities were a lot more interested and in touch with farming. And at peak times when the farming family couldn't cope with the work they would get a little team from the village they could call on. Teams attached themselves to different farms and you got a competitive element. They all watched each other to see who could get the hay in first. They were paid, and the millworkers would finish their shift in the mill in the summer and go straight to the farms.'

Young Colin Cooke never asked for any money when he and his pals helped with the haymaking in the fields around Higham. To a lad it was an honour to help out on the farm. 'If you worked on a farm you were somebody. Pay never crossed your mind.' They used to mow with horses and he remembers single and double mowing machines. When you started courting they had a saying. If you went to a dance and got off with a girl your pals would ask, 'Will she mow double?' Colin draws an enchanting picture of lads coming down off the meadow in the evening after a long, hot day haymaking. Their feet and clothes are black from the dust and they stop to slake their thirsts along with the horse in the cattle trough. The Irish labourers were given beer from a barrel of ale bought specially for the harvest by the farmer and kept cool with a damp sack in the dairy.

In the small district of Briercliffe to the north east of Burnley, historian Roger Frost calculates that forty years ago when he was a youngster there were 70 or so working farms. Now there are only around nine. The result of this change, he believes, is that the land is no longer so well cared for. Walls fall down and aren't replaced and local woodland is degenerating. But he doesn't see the same disaster as in other parts of the country where intensive agricultural methods have led to the loss of hedgerows and the growth of vast, featureless fields. We may no longer have each farmer with his own milk round clip-clopping along every back dad with a horse and cart full of milk kits and a horde of kids all eager to hitch a lift on the step at the back or help fill the jugs that were left on the back-door step of every house. But we've still got our small fields and hedgerows, leaving much of the landscape looking more or less the same as it did.

But one perceived threat to the landscape which concerned many of the people I spoke to is the spread of suburbia. Modern housing estates are steadily blurring the limits between town and country until any escape into the wilds like our ancestors enjoyed becomes a major expedition requiring climbing boots and emergency rations. If Edgar Wormwell's otter was foolish enough to return to the beck through Kelbrook it would have its retreat cut off by ranks of so-called executive homes. Artist David Wild looks on in dismay as our valley sides start to fill with 'formulaic housing

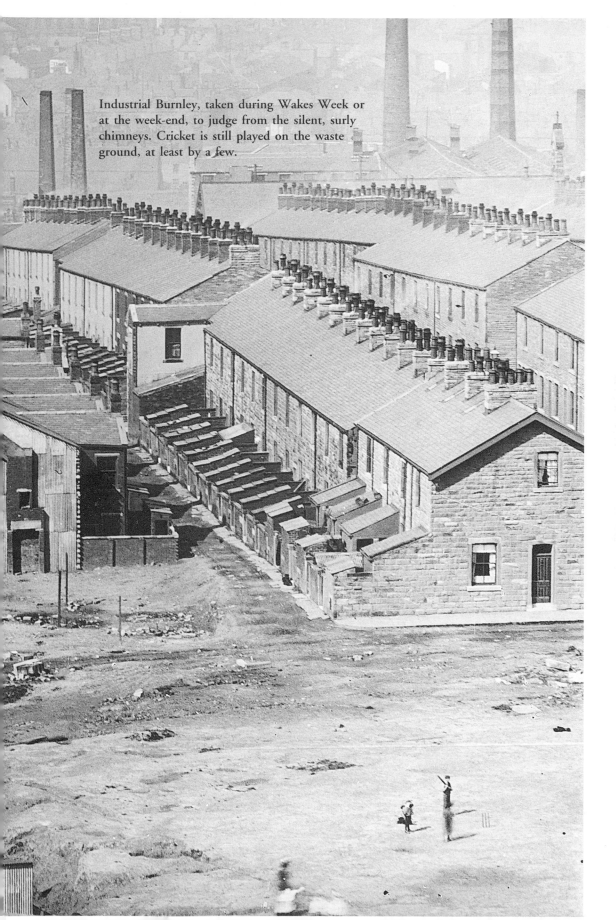

Industrial Burnley, taken during Wakes Week or
at the week-end, to judge from the silent, surly
chimneys. Cricket is still played on the waste
ground, at least by a few.

estates where everyone has a garden with a garage for two cars, and the primeval valley landscape becomes yet another urban sprawl.' Others, like Roger Frost, lament the loss of a favourite view. Jim Cropper from his eyrie up on Deerplay Moor watches the housing estates creeping ever closer. 'It's going to be like Bacup town moving to the country soon,' he says.

But to return to the atmospheric blight of the cotton mills. Today, everyone who remembers those days breathes a smoke-free sigh of relief for the Clean Air Acts of the 1950s. 'It was a great thing when we got the Clean Air Act of 1956,' says Ken Spencer. 'It made it possible for houses and buildings to be cleaned and remain clean. That, for me, has been one of the most cheerful revolutions of my life-time.'

But it seems to be the nature of the human animal that no sooner do we get rid of one problem than another raises its Hydra-like head. Ruth Collinson, a farmer's wife from Chatburn in the Ribble Valley, has been fighting pollution from the cement works in Clitheroe. She alleges that smoke from the chimney, a modern landmark in the valley, is causing health problems.

'When this smell started I didn't know what it was so I started writing it down in a diary and I actually wrote at the time, 'itchy eyes'. I didn't know why but something was affecting my health. I've always been a healthy person so I knew something was wrong. And then my granddaughter started with asthma and my son had some health problems as well. I think there are a lot of people, particularly elderly people, who have started with asthma. Why do you start with asthma when you get into your 70s? My grandson says he could taste it in the schoolyard at Chatburn School. I know that it's going up there. Sometimes I've had to shut the windows. If that had been there from time immemorial we would have known about it 33 years ago when we first came here. It's not coming from the rock. It's coming from somewhere else.'

The problems of modern environmental pollution are an insidious and persistent worry to people. Perhaps our grandparents would have brushed the soot out of their whiskers and laughed at us. Here we are on the brink of a new millennium, our satanic mills and disgraceful slums swept away; we're well-fed and lack for nothing, with every modern convenience at our finger tips, and yet we are no better than our medieval ancestors haunted by the spectre of plague and damnation. Only the demons we fear will carry us off are poisoned air and contaminated food. Ken Spencer, who is a respected ornithologist is seriously worried by the drop in our bird population:

'Skylarks are down. Meadow pipits, reed buntings, snipe, curlew and lapwing are all seriously down in numbers. The general consensus is that it's due to a change in agriculture. But I'm not completely happy with this explanation. There's something more.'

He cites the loss of skylarks from the moors above Burnley where he's been going for over fifty years but where there hasn't been any conspicuous agricultural change. There's something else, he thinks. 'It could be emissions from exhausts or something like that. But it's all speculation.'

Colin Cooke is more certain. 'They're fertiliser mad,' he says. 'And everything's sprayed – the kerbside, all our vegetables. And the day after, they're putting the same stuff on again! They'll come unstuck,' he warns. 'What goes in must come out!'

But whatever changes occur to the environment in which we live, for the Lancashire people I have spoken to one thing endures. And that's a deep and passionate love for their bit of this country.

'Stand on top of Rieve Edge above Thursden Valley,' says Roger Frost, 'and on a clear day you have a magnificent view that takes you across to Lancaster in one direction, across to Pendle, across towns like Burnley, but beyond towards the moors above Blackburn and Darwen. There are magnificent views on our own doorstep! And for Andrew Nuttall who has just renovated an ancient barn above the village of West Bradford which commands a panoramic view across the Ribble Valley, 'The main thing for me is that it looks over the drop end of Pendle, and whether it's raining, sun shining, blowing, hailing, whatever it's doing, it's the best view in Lancashire.'

Others may question his opinion, but take it from me, no one could deny his passion for where he lives.

'It were damned horrible' emptying the nightsoil.

Chapter Two

House and Home

Even as recently as the late 1950s it was possible to catch sight of the 'walking bath' in Cleveland Street in Colne. 'There'd be a bit of a rumble and the bath would be removed from its nail in the backyard and off it would go down the street on somebody's head!' The correct response to any sighting seems to have been to call: 'Bath night, Peter?' – or whoever's head happened to be inside the moving tub – to which a muffled reply would come: 'Aye, bath night.'

We are indebted to David Palmer for an explanation of this curious social phenomenon:

'I was 18 or 19 when I got married and moved to Colne. Very few of us had a bathroom but my sister who lived opposite had a tin bath and we all took turns to borrow it. There were at least 5 or 6 families in the street used it, and you knew when you saw it going off down the street that it was their turn. It went to a different house every night and it was all night of a job.'

The unashamed luxury of most modern homes brings the same response from older people reared off a weekly wash in a tin bath in front of the fire: 'They don't know they're born these days. Even half-a-century ago many Lancashire homes were so basic as to be barely recognisable from the insides of the same dwellings today.

David Palmer was brought up in a back-to-back in Barnoldswick.

'It were that basic it were unbelievable. We had a stone floor with a peg rug, a black lead grate and a slop-stone sink and this scrubbed-top pine kitchen table covered in newspaper. There were no cupboards in the kitchen, only shelves. We has a stone staircase. Dolly and Stella slept on the landing with my mother and the rest of us all slept in a double bed. Above that was an attic with a home-made ladder but no one would sleep up there because we thought there was a ghost. We had a coal bunker at the front and at the back twelve families shared four outside toilets. Though our house has been pulled down, the row still stands today and they're regarded

as extremely posh. They don't call them terraced houses any more, they
call them cottages.'

When life is pared down to such fundamentals your few possessions
become precious and must be preserved.

Weaver cutting fur for lining shuttles.

'My mother used to tie paper bags round the legs of the kitchen table to keep the dust off. And we had this old couch. I remember old Esther used to call in on her way back from the shops for a rest and a fag. One day she sat on this couch and her arse went through. My mum mended it. After that when Esther used to come she used to shout: "Don't sit on that end o' t' settee or you'll go through!" It was like that for years.'

When David looks back he's amazed that they had their own tin bath and didn't have to share it. The toilet was a different matter. There was a journey of about a hundred yards through a passage and out to the back and if someone from another house was there you had to wait. You knew when a member of your own family had gone because they kept a key with a cotton bobbin tied to it on a hook in the house and if that was missing you knew you'd have to wait.

Sunday night was bath night. David being the only lad and youngest, he had to wait while his 5 sisters had theirs. Girls or no girls the water must have been a bit murky by the time he got in. There was no question of heating fresh water. And then came the head lice ritual. Everyone's hair was washed in Derbac soap and David remembers having to sit in front of a newspaper while his mother combed and combed his hair with a bone comb. This tedious operation had its compensations for a small boy because if a louse fell out he was allowed to snick it with his thumb nail. "There's one! There's one!" his mother would cry, and David would snick it until it cracked. 'That made you suited and all the combing was worthwhile.' There then followed a post mortem as to who got them from whom. But it sounds largely academic because they all slept together.

Rituals like this were taking place in thousands of homes throughout Lancashire. Stories like them crop up again and again. They are a deep reservoir of common experience which united us all. And the same domestic objects feature in every household as means of providing the fundamental necessities of life, needs that haven't changed since time immemorial: keeping clean, keeping warm and keeping your belly full. Today, with all the sophisticated gadgetry of modern life, it's easy to lose sight of these basics. In the old days it wasn't, because a few simple things were all you had. The black-leaded oven and fire is a prime example. It warmed you, you cooked on it, and it had a boiler that provided you with hot water. So simple. Don't tell today's domestic appliance manufacturers. If someone brings them back they'll all be out of business.

Emma Edge is the oldest person I interviewed, to say nothing of her being one of the liveliest. Emma was born in 1898 and is still going strong living alone at her home in Waterfoot in Rossendale. She was brought up

Emma Edge.
At 101 years, the
oldest person
interviewed.

on a farm above Bacup and she remembers how, without gas or electricity, the black-leaded range was the centrepiece of the farm kitchen.

'In winter Dad killed a pig and he'd slice it up and put the pieces of bacon in a Dutch oven (a round metal container you put in the fire). You'd to get a good fire going before it would start cooking. The fat dripped off. We never bothered with the bacon, it was the dip butties we had. It were real good. We had an oven at one side of the fire and a boiler at the other with a tap on. Dad used to take hot water to mix with the cattle food and one day he left the tap running. When we looked the house was swilling. We had to get the mop and bucket out. We'd have played pop wi mi Dad but we daren't.'

Jim Cropper remembers flitting to their farmhouse on Deerplay Moor when he was four. Everything had to be carried a mile out on to the hills and he had to carry the mop bucket. It was good practice because when they got there they found the farm's water supply had disappeared because of underground mine-workings. Each day before they went to school and every night when they got home they had to carry water from the next farm half-a-mile away, enough for themselves and all the farm animals.

Florrie Birtwell, who is now 96, lived in a house in Wiswell near Whalley with no water. They had to go next door. When next door's water supply froze up in winter she remembers going down Barrow lane with a bucket to a well. 'It never froze over and was crystal clear. They should never have covered it up like they did when they made the bypass.' Florrie remembers blackleading the grate and putting the fire-irons down just for the weekend, the same with the Sunday rug. And then on Monday they went back under the couch until the following weekend.

It was a similar story for Lizzie Hartley of Colne. They'd to make do with a bare flagged floor all week before matting was put down on Saturday until Sunday night. They had a peg-rug which they pegged themselves. Her mother had a frame which was stretched with hessian and then they all sat round pegging strips of cut-up old clothes through it until they were tight. 'But when you came to shake it it were heavier than t' flagged floor. it took three of us to tek it out and shake it. Talk about dust!'

She remembers two double beds in one bedroom with the two boys in one bed and her and her sister in the other. Her mother and father slept in a second bedroom with the baby in a cot at the foot of the bed. This seems a relatively spacious arrangement compared to some households where it was nothing to have four in a bed top-to-tail, or 'bread-and-butter' style as John Parkinson of Blackrod rather eloquently puts it. When Lizzie fell out with her father over the man she was going to marry, she stayed for 6 months with her cousin Thyra and her family. They lived in a one-up and one-down and Lizzie had to sleep in the same room with five others on a mat, with only a clothes maiden draped with a red quilt for privacy. John Parkinson recalls people getting married during the 20s and 30s and going to the local farmer for chaff or cut straw to fill the nuptial mattress. If you were posh you bought a feather-filled flock. Lizzie Hartley remembers keeping warm as a child with a plate on her feet which her mother had heated in the oven, wrapped in an old blanket and popped in her bed. In those days in winter Jack Frost shared your house and left his trade mark patterns of leaves and crystal ferns on the <u>inside</u> of the bedroom window.

The tribulations of the toilet would fill a chapter of its own. The old iron bedsteads that everybody had were a lot higher off the floor than a modern bed. This left plenty of room underneath for the 'gusunder'. A hundred-yard journey on a cold, dark winter's night, with the wind and rain lashing off the Pennine hills and down the back street, was only to be undertaken by the most fastidious. When you did use an outside toilet, especially if it was only a soil bucket, the experience could stay with you for the rest of your life. Like it did with 86-year-old Donald Barker who lived in a village near Water in Rossendale.

'It were damned horrible! I'll never forget them. The worst thing I've known in my life. And men used to come and empty them during the day: two blokes with a big cart and a shire horse. You knew what was coming up, the stench was terrible. You'd be coming from the shops with some fish and chips or something and this were coming past. And then they'd empty it on the fields. Raw sewage. And there'd be masses of birds everywhere. Horrible!'

But in the towns people usually had a long-drop toilet with a tippler. Albert Morris from Nelson, a man with a distinct scientific bent, can recall these with rather more detachment:

'I'm not an expert but they were very interesting. They were built at the far end of the yard away from the back door with a large wooden seat with a hole in the centre. They were called long-drops because they were built about five or six feet above the main sewer. Into this was injected waste water from the kitchen sink which drained into the tippler, a shoe-shaped earthenware container which was on pivots. When it got full of water it would tip over with a rush and then a clunk as the tippler returned.'

And woe betide the nervous who were sitting there in the dark when the tippler flushed. You didn't dally much at the toilet in those days. The sides never got properly flushed and there was always a strong smell. No one ever reported anyone ever falling down but this didn't stop them from being places of terror to many a young child.

Margaret McLean was one. 'It was very frightening for a child out there in the pitch dark. No one ever thought of giving you a candle or anything. You just sat there absolutely terrified. I wouldn't have liked my children to have gone through anything like that.' She remembers the pet rabbit getting out and being chased by the dog before taking refuge down there. And cats had a tendency to disappear down them as well. According to Margaret they had a big scoop ready if anything needed rescuing.

Inside she paints a picture of domestic bliss Burnley-style in the 1950s. 'There were 8 of us, six children. The younger ones had to stand up round the table because there wasn't enough room for us all to sit down. We all squashed into this one little room. The back door was in the same room with a great gap underneath where the wind used to whistle in. You froze

Outside lavatories.

everywhere in the house in the winter unless you hovered over the fire. There was a tiny scullery with a pot sink where you got washed and it was so cold in the bedroom you put your clothes in bed with you and got dressed under the covers next morning. When everyone was at home it got very crowded. My brothers, who'd started working down the pit, used to strip off and wrestle behind the back door, shouting and screaming. We were fighting in another corner while the dogs ran around barking. Mum sat at her sewing machine blissfully ignoring all the chaos.' I don't know what modern psychology would make of the effects of all this on a young child, but if you met Margaret today you'd find a most civilised and thoughtful person.

As a real contrast to those unruly scenes in the Burnley household we could turn to the house in Leyland where Alice Whittle was brought up with her Grandma. Here's an interior out of one of those bread adverts: all warm glow and filtered firelight.

'I can still see it now. The fire in the grate, especially on bath night. Two polished pot dogs on either side, grandma in her rocking chair crocheting and the old black kettle whistling on the hob. Marvellous.'

Only one thing marred this picture of domestic contentment for Alice. 'After my bath I'd to sit down and get dried on the sofa and the horsehairs pricked my bum!'

And next door was the parlour or best room:

'You weren't allowed to go in except in your socks and even then grandma inspected them to see if they were clean. Inside that parlour was like going into magic. There were coloured tiles down the sides of the fireplace and on the mantlepiece Uncle Joe's models. Uncle Joe had a fretwork machine and one of the models he made was a Fishwick's bus. He was a conductor for Fishwick's buses. Oh, I loved that bus! But we hadn't to touch anything. On the table by the window with its thick lace curtains she had a great big aspidistra. I had to go in there with a rag with oil on it – I don't know what sort – and go over all the leaves. And grandma would come in to inspect and see that I'd touched every leaf. I can smell that room now. It was Mansion polish. And she had a stuffed bird in a globe on the table where this aspidistra was. Oh, and I tried my best not to look at it but it seemed to be looking at me! That's one thing I hated in that room, that bird.'

There's always a nightmare lurking somewhere in the corner of every childhood memory from that era. Is it the shadow of the Victorians? But what, oh what, I asked, was the point of parlours? What on earth were they for?

'Nothing,' said Alice – and now I really feel I've strayed behind the looking-glass. 'It wasn't for anything. It was shut off. Nothing was ever moved. Everything had to be in its place and if it was moved, grandma knew. It was taboo. It was like as if you could have put a card on the door saying "No Admittance".'

Could Val Thome of Nelson throw any light on this dustless domestic riddle?

'We only ever went in on a Sunday or Christmas Day or when the vicar called. On a Sunday dad would light a fire in the front room instead of the back room where we lived all week. What a stupid idea that was! The front room never warmed up until you went to bed, and then you had to go back into the dining room for all your meals which by now was cold. So you spent all Sunday completely frozen.'

An even more chilling explanation for the purpose of the front room comes from Stanley Graham of Barnoldswick.

A posh textile manufacturer's house, well upwind from the town.

'You had to have somewhere to put the body. You never buried during the week in Barnoldswick because people couldn't afford to be off work. And the Church of England didn't bury on Sunday. So Saturday was funeral day. So if someone died on Saturday in the middle of June in a heatwave you'd got to have somewhere to keep the body – on the table with the cloth draped down over the side and the bucket of Jey's fluid underneath to try and mask the smell. The front room was a good place to do it. You could keep the window open and the door shut.'

A rare glimpse into the luxurious interiors of some of the well-to-do cotton manufacturers comes from Arthur English, a choirboy at St Thomas's church in Barrowford just before the Second World War. Each year they were invited to tour the leafy suburbs of Nelson, places like Higherford and Blacko, where the mill bosses lived, well upwind of any factory smoke and the smells of less exalted humanity in the terraces. And they were invited in to sing carols at Christmas. They trailed up astonishingly long drives through gardens and past greenhouses and garages. And inside they were met by wall-to-wall carpets, thick velvet curtains, beautiful open staircases, billiard rooms full of rich leather chairs and even a minstrels' gallery. 'I'd never seen anything so fabulous in all my life,' says Arthur. 'I

Mary Cockle proudly brandishes her new jerry.

didn't think property like that existed. It was all money made out of the cotton trade.'

I don't think they run to minstrel's galleries in the terraces of Nelson today, but the gulf between the homes of ordinary people and the well-off has shrunk enormously from those days 50 years ago. Expectations have soared since the age of slopstones and walking baths, and the pride which poor people had in keeping their doorsteps scrubbed and their paintwork shining has led to, with today's greater affluence, the transformation of many a terraced house into 'little palaces.' But with today's assault from advertisers, style magazines and TV house make-over programmes reaching heights our grandparents would have regarded as madness, it's encouraging to find one or two individuals who are resistent to such changes and are content with the simple life.

Roy Ashworth, whom I met in a Salvation Army hostel in Blackburn as he waited for the weather to improve to take to the hills of the Yorkshire Dales, needs only the sky over his head to feel happy. His possessions comprise no more than he can fit into his rucksack. His freedom is what is precious to him and he doesn't want to be 'lumbered with belongings.' He's in his 60s but as comfortable in a tent as anywhere. He's slept in a rock-cut prehistoric tomb on Orkney Island. 'I thought, why put up my tent when I can stay in here. I like that sort of thing. It appeals to me, and it didn't let any rain in. Today's sophisticated life doesn't do anything for me and I just don't want it.'

But my favourite maverick is Mary Cockle of Waterfoot. She's 77 and has no bathroom and still makes do with an outside toilet. Bath night is in the kitchen standing at the sink. 'I never miss an inch,' she says proudly. 'My mother never had a bath and she lived to be 88. People are too soft these days. They want too much heat. All those showers and all that stuff they put on their bodies, I couldn't be bothered with all that sort of thing. And then she leans forward confidentially. 'I bought a new jerry the other week and the woman who sold it to me said, "It will look nice will that with flowers in." "Excuse me," I said. "This is being bought for what it was made for."'

Long live Mary Cockle! A warm, living human museum for the way we were!

A memorial to the dead of the First World War on Deerplay Moor above Bacup, close to the source of the River Irwell.

Chapter Three

Who Are We?

O<small>NE</small> O<small>F</small> the most curious omissions from the broadcast series on which this book is based is any serious attempt to measure the impact of two world wars on our lives in the twentieth century. The annihilation of the flower of youth in the 'Pals' companies of so many Lancashire towns in 1914–18, and the effects of enlistment on local families in the Second World War, to say nothing of civilians living on the margins of so much aerial destruction in Liverpool and Manchester, had a profound effect on local life. And this is all before we start to take into account things like wartime rationing, the influx of evacuees and refugees, or special wartime employment. But the workings of the BBC minds who thought up the series are labyrinthine and a mystery to mere mortals like us. Their thinking was, it seems, that 'The Century Speaks' would provide an entirely new archive to bestow upon the new millennium, and mouldering in the vaults of Broadcasting House there was already a mass of material about the war and so they didn't want any more. Forget that people tuning in, or picking up this book, might expect to learn about the part local people played in the two greatest episodes of armed conflict in the history of humanity. No, when I first set out on these interviews, the injunction 'Don't mention the war!' was ringing in my ears like an echo from Fawlty Towers. It is, of course, just plain daft to ask elderly people about their lives in the twentieth century and not talk about war. And it kept cropping up. References to the military hospital at Calderstones near Whalley in World War I and the train loads of wounded that used to go past. Tantalising questions arising out of a remark by a 90 year old who, as a schoolboy, had to collect sphagnum moss off the moors for use in the hospital. What use? For dressing wounds? What sort of wounds? You can't stop asking questions once a series like this begins starting so many hares. And then I walk into a front room in Colne to find an enlarged newspaper picture on the wall of the man I've come to see chasing up the beach at Dunkirk with the allied landings. Shall I pretend I've not seen it and talk to him about donkeystones?

Fortunately, Programme 3 asked, 'Who are we?' It is an investigation into our sense of nationality, and if war isn't about a sense of national identity and the mother country you're supposed to be fighting for, I don't know what is. Even if that fighting means never raising a rifle in anger but slinging flour bags at one another on Pendleside doing an excellent imitation of Dad's Army in the Home Guard. So here's a chance to bring down the wrath of the BBC and at least mention the wars.

But first our sense of being English or British or call it what you like, as people do. The first thing we need to recognise is, to put it bluntly, we're a bit of a bastard lot. That's the way Stanley Graham from Barnold-swick, via Stockport, is quite happy to describe himself.

'I'm not English. I'm the biggest mixture you could ever come across. My mother was English – as far as I know. But I've come across a reference to her family name, Challenger, in a man who was arrested for seditious riot in Ashton-under-Lyne in 1837. Through my father my ancestry is Scots – thrown out by the Clearances – Neopolitan – left Naples while it was a separate kingdom – German, Swedish, Irish. And my dad himself, who came from Australia, wasn't sure whether there was a bit of aborigine somewhere – I certainly go extremely brown in the sun. So when I look at my ancestry I just think it's crazy to be welded to a concept like patriotism. 'My country, right or wrong.' I feel as much loyalty towards Australia, I feel sympathy towards the Irish, I love Scotland ...'

Now here's a pretty can of worms we've opened. And when I met the Burnley student and asked her where her loyalties lay, I was told, 'Yes, I suppose I'm British, I was born here –' And then a pause and intake of breath. 'But my father is Irish, my mother was born in Kenya and my grandparents are both from India.'

Things were a lot simpler in Titus Thornber's day. Just after the First World War he remembers feeling proud that we'd won the war. He was also very proud of the British Empire. As children they used to collect British Empire stamps. 'With the cotton trade covering the globe we had an advantage because the sales offices were in Manchester. They were getting letters from all over the world and we chased our uncles and fathers to collect as many of the envelopes as they could and then we'd steam the stamp off with a kettle. We'd then look the places up on the school atlas and we felt a nice feeling of superiority when we saw that nearly half the world seemed to be coloured red. We were proud of the fact that we were the young heirs of this wonderful British Empire.'

Colin Wiseman, who is now 90 and is the one who had to collect the sphagnum moss that went to the Queen Mary's Military Hospital at

Calderstones to help the war effort, had a rather more down-to-earth attitude. The Empire didn't help him very much, he told me. 'All I knew was that there was a map and all that which was shaded red was ours. But I didn't get anything from it with it being ours. They didn't send me anything.'

Tommy Dowling, a veteran of Dunkirk and also 90, recalls being taught at school about Britain's colonial greatness.

'I used to like reading about that. The history books were always going on about the colonies we'd won. I was proud of what we'd achieved through military power. If they had any trouble they used to send a load of ships to fly the flag and frighten them to death.'

But Tommy saw things differently when he went to India and the Far East at the end of the Second World War.

'When I saw what we'd done to some of these countries, I was a bit ashamed. India was disgusting. We were stationed at Secunderabad. It had all been exploited. There were slums worse than ever there were in Colne. I remember going past in a wagon and this old man dropped down dead in the street and he was just left there.'

But for one of the most revealing insights into the inequalities of the old colonial regime, we need go no further than this country. John Holt was a young fireman on the railways in 1947 when India gained her independence. He remembers his engine coming into Euston station and seeing the passengers who had disembarked from a liner at Liverpool and been brought on to London.

'It was when the civil service left India and I remember being amazed. The platforms were railed off for them, and all these very posh people that had Rolls Bentleys waiting for them got off the train with Indian servants and nannies for their children. They had plenty of Silver Cross perambulators when we were all on ration points in this country. And they were taken away by these posh cars. They didn't look like people who had lost their jobs. They didn't seem to have to rely on unemployment pay.'

It is such obliquely-observed insights into some of the great events of the century that make an oral history series like this so fascinating and surprising. You don't always have to be at the hub of things to present a view every bit as valuable as that of the historian in his arid study or the statesman in the cabinet room. In fact, John Holt's testimony will live longer in my mind because he observes the wealth of Empire from the viewpoint of a Lancashire lad brought up amongst the unemployment of the 1930s.

Part of the old sense of patriotism came from the impression ordinary

The visit of George V and Queen Mary to Colne 9 July 1913. How many of us would scale our roofs today to get a glimpse of royalty?

people got of the majesty of royalty. Colin Wiseman saw pictures of George V in his medals and grew up thinking him to be a great soldier, which of course he wasn't. But nevertheless, he looked up to him. 'We didn't run them down in those days and scrutinise them. He was the King and I was one of his subjects.'

'When you got photographs in the newspapers of George V and Queen Mary, or as they were then, the Emperor and Empress of India, they really looked like Kings and Queens, wearing crowns and regal dresses,' says Titus Thornber. 'I must say I'm very disappointed today in that our royalty are not distinguishable from anyone else in the crowd.'

But Titus is quick to point out that he's not merely a moist-eyed royalist. It is the institution he values, with its thousand-year tradition. 'Without the stability of royalty,' he thinks, 'without its constitutional role as head of the judiciary, armed forces and Parliament, power is denied to anyone else and it would be impossible for a Hitler to take over.'

Tommy Dowling says he had a good idea of what he was fighting for when he joined up in the Second World War. He'd heard about the atrocities of the Nazis and he wanted to go. 'It was not so much a question of fighting for king and country but I was fighting for this country's families, the children. We didn't want to see the same thing happening to them as was happening in Europe.' And when the war was over and he went to Belsen, the nadir of twentieth century inhumanity, he'll never forget what he saw:

'We looked through the windows of our billet and some of the prisoners were gorging themselves off our swill bins. It was a terrible sight. And you could smell the place miles away. There were just skeletons everywhere. It was terrible.'

But today Tommy would rather have the Germans than the French. He didn't trust the French then and doesn't now. When he goes on holiday

Dad's Army.

Alice Whittle of Leyland with some of her late husband's military medals. (*Lancashire Evening Post*)

to Jersey he doesn't like them. 'I know it's wrong for me to be that way, because I'm a good Catholic, but it's something left over from the War.'

When Margaret Creamer of Rawtenstall goes on holiday, every time she sees a German she sees them in a uniform. 'I avoid them because I think I could fall out with them. I'll never forget what happened during the War. It took our youth. From 1939 to 1945 your life was gone.'

Alice Whittle remembers the sense of patriotic pride that came over her during the War. 'How could you not have that British spirit when you were part of it?' she asks. She wove parachute cloth and felt proud of what she was doing to help the war effort. She even became the factory watch at the mill in Leyland where she worked. She remembers the bombers coming over to bomb Liverpool following the railway line. She imitates the sound of the engines: the heavy menacing drum when they were loaded with bombs and how the note changed to a steady drone when they'd dropped them and were returning. She remembers a lone German bomber circling Leyland looking for the Ordnance Factory at Euxton, or else Leyland Motors. But when they fired the gun off at Leyland Motors he dropped his bombs and left. Alice remembers them landing on Ward Street at Lostock Hall right next to the factory where her dad worked:

'It was a summer Sunday afternoon and we saw this plume of smoke go up. A bomb had dropped in the street and the factory stoker, Mr Benson, had sent his daughter Alice to get him a packet of cigarettes. And there he was digging with his hands in the rubble. And to this day, God rest her, she was never found.'

As you listen to people's lives, a story like this of indiscriminate tragedy will suddenly emerge. And when the shared sense of sorrow is past you are left with a deepened feeling of respect for the way ordinary people cope with such things and go on with their lives.

But tragedy and comedy play an equal part in the human drama. Those comic heroes of Dad's Army weren't just to be found at Warmington-on-Sea. They were alive and well strutting and bungling their way around Lancashire too during the war.

'Oh, bloody hell, t' Home Guard,' cries Colin Cooke of Sabden, drooling with relish at the chance of wheeling out some of his many Home Guard stories.

He was only 16 when he joined, Corporal Pike's age, I suppose.

'If you came with shoes on and a tie you were made a corporal right away. The posh ones got the first uniforms and at first we only had two rifles so we used to toss up to see who was to carry the rifle. We used to have to guard the wireless station above Higham every night. There was no danger but we still had to guard it. The bank manager was the major right away and he used to line them up on a Sunday morning. And the farmers used to come late. They may have been calving a cow and they'd come up with a dog behind them. And they used to march down the road on parade and the dog would follow the farmer and he would be kicking it and shouting, 'Get 'ome, dog!'

'And the major used to say, 'Right, we're having manoeuvres. You two are German prisoners, you've got to escape and we'll come looking for you.' And they finished up in the pub playing dominoes. They were in all day and we were looking for 'em ... And then they reckoned to attack Burnley one day. And they were throwing electric lightbulbs at us – you know how they bang – instead of bombs. We know nowt these days, do we?'

But the comic antics of the Home Guard masked a serious concern about the threat of invasion. Alice Whittle, when she became the factory watch, was helping to defend her country. 'This country was mine, so you had a big sense of duty as well as responsibility.'

But how does she feel about her country today?

'If you really want to know, I'm ashamed of the country today. I'm ashamed of a lot that's going on and the people in it. Why has it been let go? Why wasn't it like this during the War when we had rationing and were queuing for queues? They're not short of anything these days, so why all this thieving, mugging, raping? Why all these drugs?'

Another unpleasant aspect of life today to upset Alice is racism. It's a concern expressed by many and seen by some as an inevitable outcome of the days of Empire.

'Let's face it, if our forefathers hadn't taken their country off them we wouldn't be in this situation,' argues Margaret McLean of Burnley. 'I don't know why everyone can't just get on with each other. People say that if they come to live in England they should do what we do. But do you think if you went to live in India you'd be doing everything that they do? I don't think so. You'd be trying to keep some of your own culture, wouldn't you?'

Race wasn't an issue in the late 1920s when Learie Constantine, the West Indian cricketer, came to play for Nelson. 'He was the first black person to come to Nelson,' Ken Hartley told me. 'He lived opposite Whitefield school and the children used to stand outside his house and peer through the window to try and see him.' Ken doesn't recall any racial prejudice, except for an incident when Nelson played East Lancashire. Constantine went down the wicket to shake the hand of the East Lancashire professional, Blankenburg, who was a white South African. But Blankenburg turned his back on him. So Constantine bowled him body-liners. Afterwards Blankenburg appeared in the Nelson dressing room black and blue from head to foot. Constantine would never admit to having done it on purpose but Ken Hartley thinks it might not have happened if Blankenburg had shaken hands.

Constantine drew thousands to watch his dazzling cricket. As Ken Hartley says, 'At a time of grim unemployment and cotton strikes throughout Lancashire in the 1930s, people forgot their troubles when they watched Constantine. He was a light at a time of despondency. The majority of people worshipped him.'

But today Ken Hartley sees no future for multiculturalism. He doesn't think that different races were ever meant to intermingle like they are doing today in Nelson. It's a common view I've heard expressed. Of course, it ignores what a mongrel breed we English are, as many, like Stanley Graham at the beginning of this chapter, are prepared to admit. Since native Celts mixed and bred with immigrant Romans, and Saxons with Normans, there's never been such a thing as racial purity on this island of ours. And if it's going to cause a problem with the latest immigrants from Asia, we can only look forward, with one person I interviewed, to the day when we're all a 'gentle coffee-colour.'

The young girl student I met at Burnley College can only start to become the norm as the new millennium advances. Her father is Irish and when she was fourteen her mother came to England from Kenya, from where her own parents had moved from India. 'I've always lived here, so I feel to belong,' she tells me. 'I'm British and nationality is not really an issue.'

But other students with both parents from an Asian background are not so happy. Being born here, even having a Lancashire accent you could cut with a knife, still doesn't make them acceptable to the more racist elements amongst their white peers. 'I think of this as my second home,' one girl tells me, 'because I don't really feel welcome.'

Coronation street party June 1953.

An Asian boy who was born here prefers to think of himself as a Pakistani because his parents have traditional views and insist on holding on to their roots. He speaks his parents' language at home and English with his friends. Many of the young Asians here inhabit a kind of cultural no-man's land. One girl told me: 'When we go to Pakistan for a holiday, you don't really feel welcome because they think of you as English, as being a foreigner. Here most people look at you and think, "Oh she's a Pakistani" and we're considered foreigners here. So we don't really belong anywhere.'

But today even the most English of us show little of the pride of those pre-war generations. We are conscious of our bad public image abroad, particularly the bad behaviour of the younger generation of holiday-maker and football hooligan. 'It's the yob element,' complains Val Thome of Nelson, 'that creates Blackpool wherever they go abroad.'

'You're ashamed of the lager louts in Spain,' says Diane Rogers, who has lived abroad in Germany for two years. 'The Germans look on us as though we're just louts. They really don't like us at all. They think we're loud-mouthed and ignorant. It's what we must come across as to them. You know, as hankies-on-heads, string-vest brigades.' Her sister Kath Thompson adds, 'They have this image of us as being stuck on an island, begrudgingly entering the Common Market but not wanting to have the euro. It's like we're there but don't really want to be. But that's what's wrong with the idea of Europe. We should be allowed to be different and be English and the Germans allowed to be German and the French French. I don't think we should ever be put into this big pot and compete with America. We should be English and part of Britain and that's as far as it should extend because we're too quirky.'

But for that self-confessed mongrel, Stanley Graham, it's not who you are that matters so much as where you live. The most valuable things to him are his circle of friends and his local knowledge. 'That's what enriches your life and it's nothing to do with nationalism and wrapping the flag around yourself. It's being able to say: This is my bit of country. It's my neck of the woods. And that's why I stay here, because I like it.'

Chapter Four

Belonging

Listen to elderly folk in the towns of old Lancashire and it isn't long before you hear a familiar lament: 'I don't even remember t' door being locked.' Some are realistic enough to add: 'Mind you, we never had owt worth stealing.' But even amongst a group of hardened young thieves I once spoke to in Bacup, over a decade ago now, there was a kind of honour and they insisted that they only confined their felonious activities to the estates of the 'off-comed 'uns' and they'd never steal from their own.

There's a lot about our surroundings which has bred a sense of closeness. 'We were poor,' people tell you, 'but were all in the same boat. More often than not that boat was a narrow valley with bleak and inhospitable moorland beyond. So we huddled together. Then the mills came along, and the owners, in the generous-spirited way of all cotton bosses, built our terraced houses as close together and as close to the mill as they could get them. More huddling. And then they set us to work in the narrow alleys of their mills. Further noisy, protracted and back-breaking huddling.

So, togetherness, intimacy, an inclination to share a life-story at the drop of a flat cap or shawl – and for which I'm eternally grateful for being able to do this series – was born.

Some cynics might say that this is all fiction, and that living together in such close proximity has merely bred nosiness, and it's our incurable inability to mind our own businesses that brings us into one another's backyards, or shuffling closer in the fish-queue on the market. Whatever it may be, the result is the same: a keen sense of belonging. These valleys may be damp and uncongenial for 7 months of the year and our terraces none too pretty on a November day when the clouds scowl, but to us they're where we belong. We love them and wouldn't be anywhere else.

David Palmer, who would share his tin bath with anybody, goes even further:

'Most people were poor but everyone were helpful, everybody were neighbourly. My mother's friends were genuine and if they could help they

Colne's Waterside. All living in the same street and all in the same boat.

would help. They cried together and they laughed together. But they were genuine people.'

Of course, there wasn't much room for airs and graces when everyone saw you at your loom every day all hot and bothered over half-a-dozen ends down, or else lived so close they could look straight into your scullery and catch you in your curlers. And if I sound a bit cynical myself, it's because I want to forestall any criticism that this is an over-sentimentalised portrait of ourselves as we were. But the more you listen to people, the more you have to acknowledge that everyone can't be wearing the sepia-tinted spectacles of nostalgia.

'My mother's friends were good friends. If my mother were having an upset, they'd sit down and have a cigarette and talk it over. And anyone else in the street for that matter.' In particular, David Palmer remembers Maggie Midgely on their street, who if anyone had died would come in the night and lay them out, wash them down and put pennies on their eyes. 'And she did it not for money but because she was concerned and neighbourly and grieved with whoever was grieving.'

When your neighbour's life was almost identical to your own, you lived in the same street, worked at the same mill for the same wage, had the same expectations, it must have been easier to identify, to sympathise and think when anything went wrong, 'There but for the grace of God ...'

Hettie Cunliffe, who has spent the best part of the century with the Salvation Army, remembers her neighbours in Nelson:

'Everybody were good neighbours in those days. I can't remember any bad 'uns. If anyone was ill or anything happened tragically or anything, it wasn't just one family, it hit the whole street.'

Donald Barker recalls being overwhelmed with offers of food when he was ill:

'I've seen some times when you could have had three meals in one sitting. Someone would bring you some potato pie and a bit of rice pudding. Someone else would bring you some stew or cow heel or a bowl of trip and onions.' Sometimes it was a case of kill 'em or cure 'em. 'The woman next door would bring a big jug of pigeon or rabbit soup that was so strong it would hit the back of your throat like a hammer. "That'll put hairs on your chest," she'd say.'

If doors were never locked it was probably to give easy access to the army of neighbours and friends who were forever visiting, or 'camping,' as Arthur English of Nelson puts it.

'I can't remember t'door being locked, even at night. There was my Auntie Susan and mi Grandma and all us neighbours. They'd come for an hour and talk about how t' mill was going on and whatever was going on in t' town.'

It wasn't just relatives and friends you kept your door unlocked for. There was a class solidarity which made even strangers welcome. Donald Barker, from Water in the Rossendale Valley, remembers them being laid off in the pit and the slipper works in the 1930s. Being bandsmen a few of them went busking to Burnley to earn a few coppers.

'We'd be out for two or three days in the summer. Sometimes you'd sleep outside, but somebody nearly always fit you up in a house. And the poorest people were always the best givers. We came to one in Burnley and there were six of us and this woman said, 'Is there any miners among you? Well come on in then.' And she had a big potato pie, and she said, 'It's for my husband and two lads but I'll find them something else. You get this.' And she gave us that potato pie. And that's what it was. The poor helped the poor more than what the others did.'

One of the most touching stories came from Ron Carter, the renowned Simonstone blacksmith.

'Mother would send me to the butcher to get a sheep's head – that was our weekend joint. She'd make broth and put barley in it. And I remember, sheep's heads were sixpence. As a child I never understood this, but I went to the Co-op in Ashton and asked for a sheep's head – Tom Neal he was called – and he looked at me, and he had a joint of beef in his hand and there was sawdust on the floor. And he dropped this joint of beef. He said, 'Oh dear, lad, I've dropped that now. What can I do with it? I know,' he said, so he dusted the sawdust off the meat and he said, 'Have that. Take it to your mum. I'll charge you sixpence for it, the same.' And we had this lovely joint of sirloin. It was a party for us that was. And mum had this little tear in her eye. The kindness touched her.'

The shared experience of the mill held people together. As Stanley Graham puts it: 'It happens when you get people fighting a common battle with common experiences and their survival depends upon having a cohesive social network. It's people getting together in a community to act as a safety net for others. Poor folk have to help each other out.'

In Barnoldswick where Stanley lives there were 25,000 looms and 10,000 people. 'So everybody knew what everybody else was doing. They knew what everybody else's job was and they knew the problems they faced because they had the same problems themselves. It's a walking distance town. People are passing each other on the way to work or else they're walking together. When they're in the mills they're communicating with each other all the time.'

Joan Driver was a weaver. 'If someone went to the toilet the person next to her ran her four looms for her. At breakfast everybody took their buffet and they sat with their pals at their loom, perhaps 4 or 5 of you. Lunchtime the same, or else you'd all meet up and go onto the market where they had about 5 or 6 cafes where you'd all sit round. And everybody helped everybody else. If someone was having a bad time they rallied round.'

The sense of belonging in the mills even extended as far as the machinery. They treated the looms as if they were their own. 'My mum and dad,' says Arthur English, 'used to take metal polish to work with them and polish the picking shafts, and they used to take yellowstone for the flags where they walked in the alleys. They felt a pride in the looms because they were theirs, even though they weren't theirs really.'

Arthur was literally born to the mill.

'My mother used to tell me that soon after I was born she wanted to go back to the mill. So the only answer was she took me with her and put me in a weft tin underneath the loom. And she's always said, "That's why you love the mill so much because you were brought up there".'

Born to the mill?

The common
experience of the
mill brought people
together – though
the chemistry here
doesn't seem to have
quite worked!

And there's nothing wrong with Arthur's hearing today, although when he tells a tale it's delivered in such splendid ringing tones it would silence the noisiest Lancashire loom.

The same network that linked everyone in the mills meant that jobs were easier to come by. 'Your auntie lived round the corner or your mother-in-law lived two doors away and they got you a job in the mill they worked in,' says Colin Waite, a recent mayor of Pendle and a Padiham lad. 'A lot of jobs were got this way.'

Colin and his twin brother Glyn can remember a real sense of community in Padiham, even as late as the 1960s when they were brought up. Glyn can list his neighbours in Stockbridge Road. They always got a welcome whatever door they knocked on. 'I still have this habit of knocking on a door and shouting 'It's only me' and I'll be half way down the lobby. We were fetched up on that. You knocked on the door and walked in.'

In Briercliffe, near Burnley, Roger Frost, a product of the post-war baby boom, belonged to one of the largest families in the area. He was one of eight children. A family like his drew in all sorts of friends from the area, which helped to contribute to the sense of belonging. 'But the older people were friendly, too. On a nice day they'd all get their chairs out and sit out on the back dad and have a good chinwag. There was always someone to talk to and people took their problems to their neighbours. Sometimes they didn't need to because their neighbours knew already.'

Of course, this proximity had its down side and it would be over-romanticising to pretend otherwise. David Palmer recalls almighty rows between neighbours.

'I've seen women fight, clogs into each other. They were good friends but bad enemies. If, for example, a fellow had an eye for another fellow's wife, they sorted it out between themselves. I've seen it come to really bad blows. In fact, I remember as a little lad the biggest fight I'd ever seen was between two women, and the whole street was out, shop-keepers and all. One's husband had been bothering with this other woman and she'd found out. He'd been dancing with her down t'Ivory Hall when he shouldn't have been and there was a hell of a battle. And afterwards they didn't speak for years. In fact, I wouldn't think they ever spoke again.'

And woe betide you if you stepped above your station. Doris Warburton grew up in a village in Rossendale. She had ambition and went to work in a shop instead of the mill. Such grand ideas didn't go down very well with her next-door neighbour, Mrs Ashworth. As Doris went past to catch the twenty-to-nine bus to work, long after the mills had started, her neighbour was sweeping out. 'We'll sweep the pavement for the 9 o'clock people,' she commented tartly.

What destroyed this sense of belonging which cemented the milltown communities? Bishop Jack Nicholls, who is now the Bishop of Sheffield but was brought up in the Rossendale Valley just after the war, is quite certain. We'll allow him, because of his elevated position, to quote some statistics.

'One of the interesting statistics is that in 1950, 85% of children and young people had some connection with a church. In 1990 that figure is 15%. And it's true of every organisation in the country which involves participation. The reverse of that is that before the Coronation most of us never saw a television. As the graph for the number of televisions shot up, the graph for people participating in life went down. That is probably as significant a fact as anything else that's happened in my lifetime.'

The Reverend Ian Robbins was vicar of Trawden from 1959 to 1969, a decade which saw the collapse of the cotton industry. When he went there he inherited the Whit walks, one of the most eagerly-awaited events of the rather scant social calendar before the war. Pastoral visits often involved him leaning across to switch off the television before he could get their attention. He remembers organising a procession of witness shortly after he arrived in Trawden: 'We set off through the village and it would be true to say that not a soul saw us. People had begun getting their cars and they were going off shopping in Colne and Burnley and Blackburn.'

The loss of the cotton mills, the advent of TV and the motorcar, youngsters moving away from the area for new opportunities, it would take a more exalted study than this to list all the reasons for the breakdown in community life in Lancashire milltowns. But this is not a textbook but a collection of personal anecdotes, of impressions gained sitting at people's firesides as they talk about the ways their lives have changed. Glyn Waite lists all the people from the Stockbridge Road in Padiham when he was a lad in the 60s. It reads like a roll of honour for a lost army scattered by the great social upheavals of the last decades. Phyllis Cunliffe, Myra Marsden, Mary Warren, I don't know them from Adam but I can see doors that were once wide open, lobbies that rang with the sound of footsteps, and living rooms full of the buzz of gossip, and those endless neighbourly brews of tea all gone, all quiet. Old folk now, perhaps, living alone with their memories, bewildered by change and perhaps frightened.

It's frightening to go onto the Stoops Estate in Burnley and listen to the stories of vandalism, drugs and theft, those modern scourges of urban living. One young mother told me: 'There's drugs. There's derelict houses.

Boarded-up houses on the Stoops Estate in Burnley, 1999.

I actually live on a street now where there's only 4 or 5 people on it, the rest are boarded up. So it's isolation. There's nowhere for the kids to play so they're smashing things up.'

And in a bare community centre I huddled round with a group of elderly residents who told me:

'Well, you just daren't leave your door or window open. If you go into next door's you have to lock your door. You daren't leave them open or someone will have been in and gone with your stuff.'

Henry has been burgled three times and another man has had his car stolen and twice vandalised:

'It's just an ongoing problem. There's a lot of drugs on the estate. There's no end in sight. And as far as community spirit is concerned, it's gone through the window. You're actually frightened of going in your own back garden. If you go upstairs you've to lock your doors because there are that many sneak-thieves in the area. Nothing's safe.'

Now you begin to see why the cry 'We never used to lock our doors' is so often repeated by the elderly. It's as much a cry of anguish for the state of things today and a damning indictment of our fall from grace as social creatures.

But out of the seige-like state of those who are left on the Stoops Estate emerges a new sense of togetherness. Just as the trials and hardships of the mill days drew people together, so the young single mothers help one another as they struggle to keep their heads above the rising tide of drugs and vandalism. They look out for each other:

'I watch and if I see someone breaking into one of my neighbours' I'd go out and stop them. I wouldn't let it happen and I'd expect them to do the same for me.'

They baby-sit for one another and share their problems, their skirmishes with the DHSS or Child Support Agency, or the turmoil of today's personal relationships. And community workers are doing their best to shore up the ruins of our once close-knit communities. It may indeed be a seige they're under, but at least there's human contact between them. Unlike the latest trend for executive estates behind closed walls, fitted with security cameras. As Stanley Graham points out: 'It is the antithesis of what happened and still does happen in a town like Barnoldswick. Thank God we've still got some of that left.'

Arthur Garnett revels in it still in Colne. He can still walk down the street and feel a warm sense of belonging. 'Everybody knows you in Colne. I can walk down the street and if I don't say hello to a dozen people there's something wrong.'

And Cath Howley still gets the same feeling in her home town of Burnley. 'It's not just the fact that I've lived here all my life, but my parents and grandparents have. It goes back and back. You can be walking down the street and see someone and think, 'Oh yes, I know that their Granddad used to go out with my Granddad. It's the whole community thing and I think it's very much alive and kicking in our town.'

Albert Morris photographs Sabrina on a visit to Nelson's Imperial Ballroom in the mid-1950s. Noted for her unusual figure, Sabrina used to stand against a silhouette of herself before inviting local girls to do the same to see if they could exceed her ample proportions. For the technically minded, she had a 42″ bust.

Chapter Five

Living Together

ALBERT MORRIS is a quiet, studious man with a passion for Hymenoptera – bees, to you and me. We met him earlier explaining the mechanical intricacies of the old-fashioned tippler toilet. He's the last person you'd expect to reveal that shortly after the war he found an irresistible technique for persuading pretty young mill-girls to take their clothes off and pose for glamour photographs.

'I used to interview these young women and they used to say: 'Nobody will ever see me without my clothes until I'm married.' Ten minutes later I was photographing her in the nude. I found a technique. You'd to praise them and tell them what a beautiful body they had and it's a shame that the general public can't see such a beautifully-shaped body with a radiant face. And it may even be a step towards becoming a film star – which it was in those days.'

Albert was already doing passport and wedding photographs when he found that a small magazine in Padiham called *Pin-up* was prepared to pay him for nude photographs. What on earth was happening to our small, straight-laced milltown communities, where the slightest whiff of scandal would get you talked about in the Co-op from one divi day till the next?

'The war seemed to alter a lot of things,' says Albert. 'It broadened people's minds.'

It also brought the Yanks to town and to places like Leyland. To the dazzlement of girls like the 17-year-old Alice Whittle.

'Wherever you went there were Americans and there was no shortage of nylons and you hadn't to have coupons to get toffees, which they called candy. And they were giving it to you. All because they wanted friendship. But the friendship of those Americans was something that we girls had never experienced, because our soldiers weren't like that. We were just took over.'

I can see you shaking your worldly, late twentieth-century heads and saying, 'This will all end in tears.' But innocent Alice continued to be dazzled.

'Now this here particular Saturday night I went to the Palace Theatre in Preston with my friend Lily. Now I used to stop on top of Spion Kop to put lipstick on, to be like the other girls: secret things that you shouldn't have to do. Anyway we went to the first house – Frank Randall was on. What a laugh! Anyway, as we sat there, two Americans came and sat down and offered us a cigarette, and I always remember them because they were called Camel. Lily took one but I didn't because I didn't smoke. And when we came out of the theatre they followed us and asked to walk us to the station. They gave us candy, and this one as was talking to me, Oh, he was talking about things as you only hear about! I'll never forget his name, it was Woodrow Church and he came from Ohio. He was lovely! Anyway, they asked to see us again "Just for another chat," he said. So we said, "All right, we'll meet you in Tardy Gate at 3 o'clock tomorrow afternoon." I thought to myself, "Chapel will be finished by then." Anyway, the next day the organist was ill and they asked me if I'd play. I thought, "I'm not going to get out of here for 3 o'clock, I'm just not going to do it." Anyway, I didn't. And my dad said to me when I came out of the chapel. "What were you rushing for there with the hymns?" We walked back home and Uncle Harry came to see my dad, and we had a table under the window and they sat at this table talking about work. And I heard my Uncle Harry say, "Nar then, who's coming here in a taxi?" Oh my goodness gracious me! When I looked out of that window that American was stepping out of the taxi and he'd a box of candy! Next thing my dad has opened the door. "Is this where Miss Taylor lives?" asked the American in his American twang. My dad said, "Aye it is, and what does ty want?" "Well," he said, "I've brought her these. I met her –" "I don't want to know where tha met her. Get thi self up that garden path or I'll put tha in that taxi!".'

And that was the end of that little episode of Anglo-American relations.

Fathers were zealous in their protection of their daughters' reputations. Long before the war, Lizzie Hartley's father had done everything in his power to stop her seeing her husband-to-be. And Lizzie was 24! What his motives were remain obscure. Robert was injured in the First World War after lying about his age and enlisting at 16. He was blown up and had a very bad limp after that. 'I don't want you seeing that peg-leg,' ordered her father. It was an astonishing outburst against a war hero and it makes you wonder just how widespread this kind of prejudice against the disabled was in small towns like Colne. Eventually Lizzie was thrown out of home and had to marry Robert in secret in defiance of her father.

Lynn Millard is another person who believes the war was a great catalyst

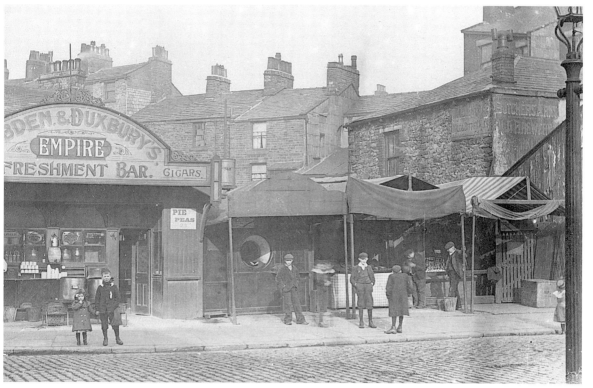

Market stalls where, come nightfall, prostitutes would ply their trade.

in beginning to bring about a liberalisation of our very rigid attitudes to sex and marriage.

'The war was a great social leveller, but, of course, it caused a lot of social problems. You had people getting married quickly before the war, before they were drafted overseas. They might spend a night or a weekend together and the man might not return for six years. Of course, he's a different fella, she's a different girl. There might have been a five-year-old child there. "Who's this man that wants to sleep with you, mum?" There were a lot of problems and this is where the separations started. And then divorce became easier.'

As a young policeman, Lynn Millard witnessed many instances of prostitution. 'I think some of the women were genuinely hard-up and had to earn a bob or two, so had to use their bodies. They never caused us any problems. We used to get a lot hanging round the market at night in the doorways. Some used to take the men home but a lot used to go on the market stalls.'

Jean Sedman remembers watching prostitutes in Nelson:

'They were ladies of the night. Good-time girls, I used to call them. At six o'clock at night they'd be waiting at the bus queue with their fully-fashioned stockings, fox-furs, all done-up, usually married women.' They had an expression in the neighbourhood for anyone they suspected of immoral conduct: they were 'not as good as she should be.' Dyed hair, particularly if it was henna, was associated with this kind of woman in Jean's book. 'They'd be out every night. They'd be off in their best clothes, their hair newly permed, wafting of Californian poppy or Evening in Paris, off down Burnley into the pubs.'

'In those days it went on but was kept under covers. Women bothered together and there were homosexuals, but they were a race apart. They didn't wear red badges and red ribbons and want rights.'

But when married relationships did go wrong there was very little divorce amongst the working class. 'Divorce was only for the toffs,' says Lynn Millard. 'It used to cost a lot of money and you usually had to prove adultery and employ a private detective. Then they had to go through the charade of booking into an hotel with a woman who was a professional adulterer. But no adultery took place. They just had to burst in and find them in the bedroom together. They would witness them sitting on the bed and those were grounds for divorce. The judge would accept it as adultery even though it was all arranged.'

Ordinary people stayed married. Joan Driver of Kelbrook says, 'You didn't pack up and leave at the drop of a hat. You stuck it out. If you were really fed up you went round to your mother's and had a bit of a moan, or we women moaned to each other. Nothing was ever so bad that it couldn't be sorted out, whereas today they give in too easily.'

The pressure on newly-weds forced to live with their in-laws must have been intolerable. Emma Edge of Waterfoot spent the first twenty years of her marriage living in the house of her husband's parents after they got married in 1925.

'Fred's mother and father were very possessive and when we married they wouldn't let him leave. I once remember being up at the pen looking after the poultry and there was a fellow there who started talking about being wed and he said, "Did I like being wed?" I said, "Jack, I didn't wed one, I wed three!" I said, "if me and Fred's falling out or having a few words, his father and mother always stick up for him." Fred still had to cough up his wage to his mother and they also had to pay rent. When she had a child, Emma had no say in what he was to be called. Her mother-in-law insisted that he was to be called Arthur after her own husband. But the child was stillborn. 'And my first words when I came round were, "Thank God! I wouldn't have been able to manage. He wouldn't have been my child. They'd have been the boss".'

Sometimes, when you hear these stories you find it hard to believe that the people are talking about life on the same planet, let alone in the same century. It can be a depressing experience listening to examples of such inhumanity and it's a sharp reminder of the shadows that hung about the 'good old days'. Nowhere was the shadow so cruel and sanctimonious than in the matter of sexual morality and teenage pregnancies.

'I don't remember any single parents,' says Pat Berry, who grew up in Nelson in the 1950s. 'If you got pregnant you got married. And girls went to homes and they had their babies taken off them. I remember talk about that sort of thing.'

'We were frightened of doing it,' says Kath Dawson. 'You went out with a boy,' agrees her friend Joan, 'and you might go six months with him before he got to kiss you in those days, let alone jumping into bed'. 'You'd bring shame on the family if you got in that state,' says Kath. 'I can only ever remember two single parents in Colne in the late 1950s, and everyone knew them. But you still didn't talk about it. It was frowned upon, so nobody said a lot.'

A modern psychiatrist would have a field day exploring the effects of all this sexual reticence and emotional repression. Val Thorne's relationship with her mother is very revealing. 'I don't remember any cuddles. I read a book once, one of those help-yourself things, and it asked you to think back to when you were small and you were held in someone's arms. And with me there's nothing there. There isn't anything there. I don't remember anyone ever cuddling me. In fact, she used to leave me alone in bed when the German bombers came over. That's something I can't forgive her for. She used to tell me. We had a cellar and she said, "I used to leave you asleep in your cot upstairs and go into the cellar because I didn't want you waking up crying." How could you do that?'

Boys were expected to demonstrate the manly virtues from a very early age. Edgar Wormwell's dad was a stonemason and Edgar can remember his hands being full of cracks and deep cuts. 'He used to have me holding a candle to drip red hot resin into them to seal them up. I used to do that regularly in the winter months. They had to be hard in those days.' And when it came to poor Edgar's turn to suffer, he had to display a similar stoicism. 'I'd never to cry. I once remember running up the steps at the chapel and I fell and broke my arm. Coming home I was crying and he started ranting and railing at me and he made a dash to grab hold of me.

so embittered by betrayal that she feels she will never be able to open up to another person ever again.'

Cath Howley, once a single teenage mother and now the mother of a daughter who is herself a single mother, can only shake her head and say:

'I think it's sad. People don't have to make any effort to be together nowadays. I won't push my daughter to get married because I'm wary now about this love thing. You think love conquers all but it doesn't, it conquers nothing at all. It doesn't last all that long. You've got to have a lot more.'

But Margaret McLean can be optimistic about one thing. We have at last got rid of the dreadful stigma of illegitimacy. Pregnant girls forced to marry or sent away to lose their children is a thing of the past. 'That was terrible,' says Margaret. 'I like today in the way that people don't have to suffer like they had to because they can talk to somebody now. It isn't hidden away any more and they can now get help. So if they don't have to suffer it means that vicious circle can be broken for future generations.'

And Cupid can still play his tricks on us, even when we get old – with the help of modern dating agencies. Barbara was 66 when she advertised for a man. He appeared in the shape of a 74-year-old who slept in his underpants and a string vest. But she found out too late and they were married. She now christens him 'the Rat' and the marriage is over. 'They think just because I've had 6 children that I must be sexy. I don't want that, I want their company. I don't mind a kiss and a cuddle but that's all. I don't want anything else. I've had enough.'

Chapter Six

Crime and the Law

$\mathcal{T}$HE chapter headings in this book follow those used for the themes of the BBC local radio series. They in turn were handed down by those BBC mandarins determined to see uniformity prevail, and the whole nation sitting down on a Sunday at noon to hear each local radio station offer identical fare: the radio equivalent of roast beef and Yorkshire pudding, perhaps. But, as grandma will tell you, there's more than one way to cook a roast, and as for Yorkshire pudding – well, everybody's got their secret recipe. What other radio stations served up, I'm afraid I don't know, but Lancashire folk expecting to hear tales of gruesome murders and grand larceny, or expecting me to extract prison stories of hidden loot, would have been disappointed. I prefer to leave that stuff to Nick Ross and his colleagues. For me, the programme gave an opportunity to dwell not upon the more lurid and sensational crimes which our daily newspapers are happy to salivate over, but to concentrate on those shifting standards of honesty and behaviour that give rise to so much anxiety, particularly amongst the elderly, so that there's a general perception that as the century comes to a close 'things have got a lot worse.' It is for this reason that I shall be returning to the theme of community and looking at the way community breakdown seems to be responsible for so much crime of the sort that affects us all today: the theft of property, vandalism, violence and drug-taking.

Compared to today, our grandparents lived in a time of undoubted innocence. Once more, the cry 'We never used to lock our door,' seemed to ring out every time I switched on the tape-recorder in an elderly household. Eddie Hothersall from Colne, whose laughter seemed to ring through the radio series like a stream of bubbling spring water, captures some of that innocence.

'There were no burglars or owt like that. You didn't even bother locking up at night. I delivered milk. I had a gallon kit with a measure and the jugs were on the doorstep and the money. Money on the doorstep in the

Windybank in Colne where the policemen always had to walk in pairs.

back dad! And in a lot of houses you just walked in. The jug would be on the table with a biscuit or apple for you. People were different then. They were nice.'

Alice Lambert, now aged 90, remembers walking regularly through one of the most notorious areas of Colne – Windybank. But nevertheless, she's quite adamant, 'In those days they wouldn't harm you.' She recalls going on holiday to the Isle of Man and leaving her door open and returning home to find everything just as she'd left it.

'You could leave t'door open and go up t'street, do your shopping, go round to t'Co-op, and nobody would go inside and pinch owt ...'

But before the image of this age of innocence has chance to take shape in the mind, before the storyteller draws another breath, the picture is shattered. The tense has changed from the past to the present and you are

A barge on the Lancaster Canal *c.* 1900 – typical of the one John Parkinson was brought up on.

hearing the words '… but you can't do that today. Nowadays you daren't go next door without locking up.'

The same realism that reminds you of how things have fallen off today is quite ready to acknowledge that in the old days they rarely had anything worth stealing.

'Everybody were in t' same boat. You couldn't pinch nothing off nobody. They had nothing to pinch,' admits Edgar Wormwell of Earby. And then his voice is lowered, as befits the recitation of an act of the most heinous criminality: 'I remember an uncle of mine had a farm and he had a hen that laid away. And he left 'em a bit before he collected the eggs. And when he went down, the lot had gone! And coal, sometimes people used to nip into other people's coal-houses and nick a few shovels full of coal. It would be all round the village. Someone's had some coal pinched!'

Arthur Garnett admits that there were some bad elements in the community. But to bring them back into line they were excluded until they'd mended their ways. 'Some bad 'uns, but we tried to sort them out. We just left them out a little bit and made them realise that they were missing out, so they became part of you.'

Over in central Lancashire, canalman John Parkinson recalls the methods for correcting wayward youngsters.

'If you did owt wrong you'd besmirched the family name. So I used to go home and get a clobbering from my dad. My grandfather didn't live so far away so he'd give you another go. So there was no way you were going to go wrong, otherwise you'd have cauliflower ears for ever. There were no gentle taps and none of this psychology of just give 'em a gentle talking to. Oh no! It was a good piece of leather. No messing about.'

And it wasn't just parents and relatives who 'corrected' the young. Other members of the community had a licence to clip ears. They also acted as informants. 'If I saw a neighbour outside,' says Joan Driver, 'and I hadn't spoken, they told your mother and you got a clip for that: "Don't you ever walk past Mrs So-and-so and never speak!" But if you were doing something amiss, a neighbour wouldn't hesitate to give you a crack. What's more, you daren't go home and tell your mother because you'd have to tell her what you'd done and you'd get another crack for that.'

'Everybody and anybody was your mother and your father in a way,' concludes Joan in a doctrine of communal responsibility which is as removed from modern thinking as most of the Ten Commandments.

Wickedness amongst children seems to have boiled down to little more than mischief. 'I mean, I were a bit of a devil,' confesses Donald Barker, from Water in Rossendale, who is now 86. 'But I never did any damage. I tied plenty of door-knockers together and upset a dustbin or two but never did any damage like they do today. And as for breaking a window, well it was unheard of was that.'

A list of childhood pranks follows which modern parents will revile me for exhuming. There was knock-and-run and window-tapping on a neighbour's window with a button fixed to a length of cotton. There was something called burglar's knock, which involved breathing on a window before running your forehead down it until it squeaked, bringing the occupant dashing to the door. Eddie Hothersall can hardly stifle his glee as he remembers tying two door-knockers together before knocking on the doors and hiding to watch the two neighbours struggling to open their doors. But his greatest jollity is reserved for the memory of the drawing-pin trick. We used to put a drawing-pin on the sneck of a yard gate and then smear it with dog-muck. And when they pricked themselves, first thing they did was to put their finger in their gob.' Eddie pulls a face before exploding with mirth. And, to show that at 74 he's still not lost his appetite for mischief, he reveals the name of the arch culprit of this trick, pointing out that he's now a big-wig at the local Methodist church.

But my favourite prank is bogey-up-a-drainpipe. This comes from David Palmer of Barnoldswick and belongs to the days of cast iron drainpipes.

Waterside – another notorious area of Colne.

They'd get a roll of newspaper poke it up a drainpipe and light it before disappearing. It roared away and sounded like a nest of demons was running amok to the unfortunate householder inside.

No doubt the elderly residents, when they'd recovered from their palpitations, shook their heads and forecast the imminent collapse of civilisation, and maybe we should remember this before we demonise the youth of today for what they get up to. The morality of acceptable behaviour has shifted as much as hemlines in the twentieth century and the police seem to have responded accordingly. Behaviour they wouldn't deign to get out of their patrol cars for today was being diligently prosecuted in the days of the police bicycle and capes.

Muriel Blenkinsop, who was born in Bolton at the end of the First World War, remembers boys of her age being fond of swinging on the arms of gaslamps. This was guaranteed to bring the law pedalling furiously in their direction. Such was the respect – call it what you will – for the police that if they saw a policeman coming they'd disappear no matter what they were doing. And the policeman's sanction was not so much his notebook but an article of clothing – his cape.

'They always carried a cape,' says Eddie Hothersall. 'It had a thickish collar and a clasp to fasten it. Well, they were pretty heavy. And it was amazing, it was always that part that hit you on the shoulder when they struck you with it.'

'There was no question of a summons, court and trouble. It was just a question of a damned good hiding with his raincoat,' recalls David Palmer, who was caught riding his brother's motorbike at 14. 'Then he went down to see my mother.'

A lot of police time seems to have been spent dealing with drunkenness, particularly at the weekends. As Eddie Hothersall remembers:

'We used to go up to the top of Exchange Street on a Saturday night to watch the bobbies wheeling the drunks on the trucks down Colne. The men had been in the pubs and clubs throughout the town – there was nothing else for them to do – and the bobbies had these two-wheeled trucks, like a barrow, and they wheeled them down to the lock-up. They put them in the cells until they'd sobered up. And that was it. They'd come out the following morning and go home.

Mary Warren's dad wouldn't let her walk through Waterside, another notorious area of Colne, on a Sunday. There were a lot of pubs down there and there'd be a lot of men that were drunk.

According to Eddie Hothersall, when you were drunk it was fair game to have a go at a policemen. 'It was the highlight of a Saturday night for some to beat up a bobby. So the police always went down Windybank in twos'. This is a sock in the eye for my theories of pre-war innocence. He does add, however, that in those days the bobbies could handle themselves. 'They were handy lads. They didn't mess about. One I remember was tall but only slim with a sallow complexion, but I don't know how many belts he had – black belts and all colours. He could tackle anyone and everybody knew.'

When they weren't demonstrating their wrestling skills or wheeling away barrow-loads of drunks, the police seem to have been preoccupied with vagrancy. Lynn Millard was a policemen in the 1940s in Burnley and remembers how they used to patrol the local 'spike' which was the casual ward at the General Hospital where the vagrants used to sleep. 'We used to check there night and morning to see who was in because of travelling criminals. We just used to turn them over while they slept. It was surprising how many people you caught.'

When a vagrant died, often overcome by coke fumes whilst sleeping in an unlocked church or school boilerhouse, it was the police job to collect the body. The police surgeon often acted as a pathologist. But if it was a case of suspected murder they used to call in the Home Office pathologist who lived in Bolton.

But murder was about as rare as a cheerful undertaker. When it did occur it was talked about forever. Joan Driver remembers a murder in Colne as late as the 1960s. The boy who found the body came into her shop a week later. 'He was only 13 but he looked like a little old man, he was so wrapped up for shock.'

However, there was no shortage of instruments of murder about, according to David Palmer of bogey up a drainpipe notoriety. He recalls that you could join the cubs or scouts and go out and buy a dagger. 'I had a scout dagger in my belt and other lads had, but I never heard of anyone being stabbed with one. Never.'

A lot of policemen's time seems to have been taken up by what we would today regard as trifles; on the look-out for horse-and-cart drivers asleep at the reins, even though his horse probably knew the way home like the back of his own fetlock. Catching boys without lights on their bicycles. I remember one burly policeman coming to our door when I was a lad and demanding to inspect our dog licence. We were made to feel that the Tower of London awaited us if we hadn't have had one.

John Parkinson remembers how they always used to have a look-out when the men were playing pitch-and-toss in the fields of central Lancashire. 'Gambling for money wasn't allowed in the 1930s and if they'd got a good pitch-and-toss school they would pay kids to keep a look-out.' His wife, Hilda, remembers the police coming for her father one Sunday after they'd caught him playing cards in the fields. They took him away and gave him a good talking to. It must have made a big impression on the infant Hilda because she says she's never liked the police since. And John is scathing about police patrols these days. 'We had a sergeant and three bobbies and they did a beat up and down the village so they knew what was going on and they knew the local villains. Today they don't know who are the villains if they're driving past in a big Bedford van, whereas the old bobby on his big sit-up-and-beg bike knew them, and any crime that was committed in the village he had them.'

Confidence in the modern police isn't high amongst many of the people I've spoken to, especially when it comes to dealing with break-ins and the widespread drug problem. Drugs have been around in the local communities since the 1960s. One middle-aged mother told me:

'You could go anywhere and get them: coffee bars, colleges, even the bus station: anywhere you wanted to go. It was who you knew, you didn't have to be anywhere special. You'd just meet somebody on a scooter outside the library or somewhere. It was growing very, very fast, so it became a money-making thing rather than a fun thing. So you got strangers moving in from out of town. It involved crime too – breaking into chemists shops stealing barbiturates or moving into hospitals where girlfriends were nurses. It was beginning to get dangerous because they were pursuing any avenue to get the drugs.'

But today's drug scene horrifies the same person now. There are stories of them being available at the school gate. I was told: 'They're in sweet form now and in little tablets that have pretty pictures on that are available to children in Junior schools. It's a big business. They're out to get as many people as they can as early as they can.'

In a community centre on the Stoops Estate in Burnley I spoke to some 10- and 11-year-olds. Their young lives are surrounded by the squalid detritus of drug use and users. One 10-year-old told me:

'They always hang around the brook and when we got down to play we keep finding needles. And outside the garage when I went to the shop, there was a drug-needle under a tree ... It's really bad and we want them to stop. It's really spoilt round here. There's nowhere to play, there's just bad-habit people everywhere.'

The elderly on the estate live in fear of crime and break-ins from young addicts stealing to feed their habit. I was told, 'The police know where a lot of the suppliers are and every so often they have a round-up. But within two or three days they're back on the streets again.'

It's not just poor families who are affected. One mother spoke of someone she knew; 'They came from a very comfortable and educated family but their son started dabbling in heroin and became addicted. And then they were wondering where their money was going and their ornaments. And that was a member of their own family. Once they've wiped out what they can get in their own family and people get wise to them, that's when they start to go to other people's houses and burgle.'

From a situation 50 years ago when the disappearance of a few shovels full of coal from a coal-house was a village scandal, we've progressed to a situation where in relatively small neighbouring towns nothing's safe:

'You can't put washing out on a washing line without it going. I had a pair of Levi jeans nicked. I was livid. I could have kicked myself because

I should have known. My child's bike was stolen when she was two. People just see things and they take them. My sister got burgled just before Christmas. They stole everything: PCs, jewellery, all sorts, and the guy opposite them had the stuff. But he said, 'Oh, I just bought it,' and nothing was done. When you do get burgled the police do absolutely nothing. I got burgled, and I thought, "Right, they'll take finger-prints and everything." No. "Just fill that form in." And that was it.'

'Today, people see things that they want and they take them. They think they have a right. If you've got something they want they don't give it a second thought, they've no conscience about it. I once knew a lad who robbed houses and I said to him, "Does it not bother you that you take people's things?" And he said, "No. All I want is my smack and if I burgle someone I don't have a conscience. I just don't." I couldn't begin to try and put some morals into him. And that's the way that people are.'

But some worry about the ever-growing appetite for violence in our communities. One mother with three boys told me:

'They laugh at me in our house because sex and debauchery I'm not bothered about. It's violence I don't like. I'll go in and turn the television off and they'll say "Why did you do that?" And I'll say, "Because I don't like the way they're all killing each other and cheering." And having boys, they're fighting like mad all the time. They're always hitting each other. And these are children who have been showered with love and affection, and all they're into now is seeing how quick they can thump each other without anyone seeing. Even in church the other Sunday, the priest nabbed one and said, "I saw you thump your brother from the altar." He said to me, "You don't mind me saying anything, do you?" And I said, "No. You can wallop them as well if you want".'

It's a strange irony that we can worry about violence in today's crime-ridden society and yet the elderly, brought up in the days of relative innocence, swear that it was the threat and regular administration of a good hiding that kept them on the straight and narrow. On the Stoops Estate, for example, they're convinced that a good beating never did them any harm and a return to corporal punishment today would rid them of all their social problems at the drop of a stick and they could all return to leaving their doors open again.

Of course, few modern educators or responsible parents would agree. It's a complicated problem with many causes about which we can speculate. My own feelings are, after listening to so many elderly people extol the trouble-free communities of the past, that a sense of closeness, where individuals kept an eye on one another within a close-knit community, is

Is it the death of the old sense of community which is responsible for so much of today's crime and vandalism?

undoubtedly a recipe for a crime-free and happy society. But the potential influences for harm from today's films, television and the media, and the rampant forces of modern consumerism, were things our grandparents never had to contend with and they tend to muddy the waters as far as any easy answers are concerned.

But to keep things in perspective, I'll end with the words of Margaret McLean, a Burnley mother whose family are nearly all grown up.

'I still think to this day that there are a lot of nice children and it's just the odd few. But they get all the publicity. So it can seem like the whole place is horrific. But I don't go along with that thinking. My son's friends are all teenagers and they're all nice lads. And I have faith that most people are nice and it's just a few who are rubbish. And that's how it's always been. But I used to say to mine: "If you fly with the crows you'll get shot with the crows." You have no guarantee that they're going to turn out all right. It just needs one little slip for them to go down the wrong road and get in with the wrong company.'

⤳ *Chapter Seven* ⤲

Growing Up

OVER THE CENTURY children have gained their freedom but lost their innocence. Half-time working in the mill at twelve, full-time at fourteen; roped in to work on the farm when you were old enough to lead a cow – deemed around five by most Pennine hill-farmers; looking after baby sisters and brothers when you were little more than a baby yourself – these were the chains of childhood servitude before the war and into the 1950s in some cases. But, nevertheless, when they were free to play, it was around cosy gaslamps in traffic-free streets at traditional and fondly remembered games which cost nothing but a bit of ingenuity. Then there were forays into the countryside, fearless of strangers, to camp and swim or 'hedge-and-dyke' and grow-up into a knowledge of the natural world around them in pre-lapsarian innocence. All long before the modern serpents of videos and video games, designer clothes and sexual precociousness crept into the school playground and destroyed it all.

'It was fun,' says Ron Carter, born in the last year of World War I. 'We were poor but life was fun. We were wild and we made our own fun. We used to play games in the street. I had an amazing childhood.'

Ron relished the physical games they used to play. They would play 'whip', a sort of hide-and-seek. And 'more weight', which involved two gangs forming a human chain and then jumping on one another's backs until the chain collapsed. 'When we got a bit older, we played 'peggy'. They called it peggy in Ashton-under-Lyne but they probably played the same game all over Lancashire. You whittled a bit of wood about two or three inches long until it had a little nose on the end. And you'd stand the peg on the floor and the nose stuck out so that if you struck it, it flew in the air. Then you caught it on the way down with an old picking stick from the looms and drove it as far as you could.'

Ingenuity was always the key word. If they played cricket they had to make their own bats by whittling a piece of wood with a penknife – a lot of whittling went on in those days and a lad without a penknife was like

Guttersnipes.

a fish without fins. Arthur Garnett of Colne was a master whittler. 'I used to help an old fella who used to bundle up firewood. He used to chop the sticks then twist wire round the bundles and I used to help him. He would give me some choice bits of wood and I used to sit on the side of the kerb carving little aeroplanes. All for nothing. You didn't have to have money.' And Arthur, still a child at heart at 69, has a model shop in Colne where he's still to be found sticking and painting – and whittling, for all I know – model planes and trains and things. The Child is father of the Man.

Girls played hopscotch or running home without treading on a nick: 'If you tread on a nick you'll marry a brick and a beetle will come to your wedding' – or a blackjack would be the uninvited guest if you were a child in Ashton. Barbara Robinson, who was born in Blackpool but spent her early childhood in Manchester, played lots of street games. 'We didn't have our heads full of materialistic things, everything was simplified. If you had a skipping rope or a couple of balls to play with against a wall or a top and whip, you were happy. We used to spend hours playing marbles and come in with our knees filthy with crawling round the pavements and you used to get a rollicking. When they had the old gaslamps with the arm on it, we used to get a rope and tie a knot in it and put a cushion over the knot, throw the rope over the arm of the lamppost, walk round the lamppost with it then push out with our feet and 'twizz' round, as we used to call it. We used to spend hours doing that. Then we would skip with a big rope stretched right across the street, six or eight of us skipping at once and singing, 'Jelly on a plate, jelly on a plate, wibble-wobble, wibble-wobble jelly on a plate!' and as we wibble-wobbled we would swing our hips from side to side.'

Girls in white ankle-socks with their skirts tucked into navy-blue knickers, long ribboned plaits bobbing around on their backs, freckled noses screwed in concentration. An enduring image of post-war street life from my childhood.

But all this ingenuity – poverty being the mother of invention – was important to Bill Heslop of Baxenden. He was brought up on a farm at

Arthur Garnett today. Still a child at heart in his model shop in Colne.

Child labour.

Shore, high above Todmorden. 'You did all sorts of things with your fingers. We used to make little waterwheels out of syrup tins and put them on every well where the water used to flow in. You were learning to use your fingers and your imagination. We made our own sledges in the winter and we made catapults. You never bought one but you'd use a bit of inner-tube from a car tyre and a leather pouch from the tongue of an old clog and a stick from a tree. And I think you got more fun making them than you did using them.'

My favourite example of such resourcefulness, something to make Robinson Crusoe proud of, came from Ron Carter. They used to tear off the street advertising hoardings and – quite the best use for adverts I've ever heard of – made then into tents. 'After they'd pasted many on, they might sometimes be half-an-inch thick and they'd be twenty feet long some of them. Well, we used to tear these placards off and go and camp. If you bent it in the middle and put stones round the side, you got a tent. And we'd be there brewing tea in an old dixie can from the First World War and we'd drink this horrible tea made of smokey water. And cut a loaf of bread with dirty hands, plastering the butter on. It was wonderful! Exciting!'

'And we made our own bow and arrows from willow: get a nice straight piece of willow and tie a piece of jinny bant – that was the string that drove the little spindles that spun the yarn – from the mill and make your bow from that. And if you whittled a piece of wood down and put a bit of wire on the end you could send an arrow out of sight.'

Arrows out of sight. Like the past winging its way into oblivion. Suburban sprawl hadn't snitched every acre in those days and there were plenty of secret hidden places close to town. I remember them when I was a lad: Bailey's field where we had our bonfire and had a den in the middle for weeks before Bonfire Night. The Devil's Tree up on the park side with its secret hollow under the roots. The narrow Pennine valleys contained the towns, the urban mess, so that the country, real wild country, was only a short walk away. Pat Berry remembers a field at the back of her house in Nelson being used for growing wheat during the war because of the food shortage. 'When the harvest came we used to build dens out of the sheaves and have the time of our lives. We used to see harvest mice and there'd be poppies. It was a child's paradise until Uncle Joe used to come along and shout, "Your mother will have no bread if you don't leave those sheaves alone!" '

We might have lived in the town but we were all country kids at heart in those days. Picnics with a bottle of Spanish water and a few jam butties – it's easy enough to parody these days, but it was such an uncomplicated and universal experience to a Lancashire child brought up before the family saloon whisked kids off to Camelot for a day out costing a month's wages to a weaver, when a treat was a gusty scramble up Pendle Hill and not a visit to the sterile confines of MacDonalds.

But shades of the prison-house soon began to close on children in those days. The late Jack Webster was born at Walmer Bridge near Preston, but the family moved to the cotton mills of Colne before World War I. Jack was twelve years old in May 1915 when he began half-time working in the mill for 3s. 6d a week:

'No option. I'd lost three brothers in the war and I had to go into the mill and earn something. My education came to an end. The half-time teachers didn't bother: we were here one week and gone the next. And when you'd been up since the crack o' dawn working in the mill, and you got into a nice warm classroom in the afternoon, you were soon nodding off. By 13 I'd started full time, 56 hours a week. Now what does a lad do when he's 13 and he's working 56 hours a week? Well, he can't get into any mischief before he's going at 6 o'clock. And when he comes home at night he's too tired to think about anything. So that was it. Childhood gone.'

For Evelyn Holt-Horsfall of Walsden, the slavery began even earlier on her father's farm.

'What I can remember vividly is, at 5 or 6 years old, having to get up early in winter time with my sister and go down into the mistal, some call it the shippon, and let the cattle out one at once to go and drink at the well. And I was terrified of cows at that age when I'd to put my arms round their necks and undo the chain and then fasten them up again. We cleaned them out as well, swilling it out. And then we'd to fill the big flat-bottom feed buckets and put them behind the cows ready for father to feed them during milking. And we'd all that to do before we went to school. And in summer-time we used to drive them in from the fields. From 5 or 6 up to 14 years old we had all this to do. And in the evening my sister and I used to have to do the milkround. And then, thank Goodness, the Government decided that no child under the age of 15 was allowed to work like that, deliver milk, without a certificate, and father was too greedy to buy one, so it stopped that, which was lovely.'

If you were an elder sister you soon became a surrogate mum. Hettie Cunliffe was only six, but her duties were quite clear:

'My mother used to start work at six in the morning and she used to waken me up and wrap the baby in a blanket and bring it into bed with me. And my brother was asleep in his cot. And I couldn't go back to sleep anymore. I had to stop awake because I'd have to get up, have my own breakfast, carry the baby to next-door-but-one to be minded, dress my brother and give him his breakfast and take him before I went to school. At dinner I used to come straight home from school, put the dinner on to warm, and then I'd go and bring my brother and the baby in and dish the dinner out while my mother fed the baby. Then at 4 o'clock I'd to do it all again; light the fire and set the table for tea ready for my mother coming home at half-past five.'

What drudgery for a 6-year-old, you think. But there's no resentment as Hettie looks back now at 90. 'I had a happy home, a happy life. We had a lot of love.'

Joan Driver was evacuated from Manchester to Colne during the war. She was two-and-a-half.

'We were all dumped in the Municipal Hall and people used to come and pick a child. Well, of course, at two-and-a-half no one wanted me. And I actually went to this family who weren't obliged to take anyone because they were too old and he'd been mustard gassed in the First World War. Anyway, the lady who became my mum had come up with her next door neighbour and she saw me and she told me afterwards: "It had got to about ten o'clock at night, but you wouldn't have anything to do with me. You were there with your pixie hood and little snotty nose, and I kept trying to talk to you. Anyway, I persuaded them to let me take you for the night." And I never went back. I must have settled in and they kept me. Then at seven, after the war, I went back to Manchester. But I never settled. I fretted and kept being ill and the doctor told my parents, "You'll do no good with her." Now they always say, "Give me a child for the first five years of its life and it's mine," don't they? Anyway, two years later I came back home to my adopted parents. Don't misunderstand me, I always went back to Manchester. I'd two sets of parents, but I never called my real mum and dad anything but May and Ernest. But I'd love from both ends.'

Joan's friend, Kath Dawson, was bringing a baby brother up at 12 years old. He was only 4 months old when their father died and her mother had to go out to work. 'You learnt from your mother. I was washing nappies, even doing the baking. These things were passed on. I bake with my granddaughter now.'

Children may have been expected to do an adult's work but they were protected from the facts of life with an almost puritanical zeal.

Ethel Howarth, brought up in Clayton-le-Moors, didn't know anything about the arrival of a new baby into the family, even though she was 11. She found out from a more worldly schoolfriend. 'She must have known about babies. She'd look at my mother and think, "She's going to have a baby." But we didn't.'

Elaborate ploys were undertaken to preserve childhood innocence. Muriel Blenkinsop remembers being taken up into her mother's bedroom and the new baby being lifted out from under the bed to encourage the belief that this was where babies really came from.

The only sex education Alice Whittle of Leyland had was off her grandma.

'My hair was my crowning glory. That's why I got all my boyfriends. But I can remember going on my bike to my grandma's on a Saturday, and she'd say to me, "Now turn round." That was to see my hair. "You're a bonny lass. Now think on, you're home for the time your dad says." And as I'm passing her rocking chair to go out, she'd say, "Na has ta getten that safety-pin in your knickers?" And that was the sex education.'

I still can't work out whether the safety-pin was to keep the knickers firmly on or for repelling any boarders. Alice continues:

'And I remember when I was courting Norman (her future husband). He was coming home on leave and my grandma said, "I want a word with you. Don't let Norman give you too many kisses." And I said to her, "Why, grandma?" "Ah well," she replied, "You could have a baby." And do you know, when Norman used to kiss me I used to think, well that's three, that's enough now.'

'And my grandma used to say, "Now, what sort of bloomers have you got on?" And I had some French knickers, and she said, "I wish you wouldn't wear them. They're not nice." And one day she went to Miss Higham's shop at the bottom of Cook Lane, it was a draper's, and I remember her giving me a brown bag. "Don't open 'em now, open 'em when you get home." And I said, "Oh, thank you, grandma," thinking perhaps they were stockings. Do you know what they were? They were a pair of navy-blue bloomers with elastic round the legs. And on Saturday night before I went out grandma asked me if I'd got them on, and I had.'

In the 1950s, there was sex education, of sorts, in schools for teenage

A class from Park School, Colne, at around the turn of the century.

The cares of adulthood already written on many of these young faces.

girls like Val Thome. It took place in the biology class and Val remembers it vividly.

'We were told, "Next week we are going to do human reproduction and there's to be no giggling. Anyone who giggles, boy or girl, will be sent to the headmaster." So fear was put into us a week ahead and we obviously weren't going to ask any questions. And I didn't know there was anything to giggle at because I knew nothing about it anyway. My mother had said, "There are two things to remember in life: never listen to girls who are talking behind the shed and never let a boy put his hand up your knickers." So those were the two rules for life and I obeyed them.'

'So we had this lesson about human reproduction, and I had this friend who I walked home with and we were in shock. She was crying and she said, "Is it true?" Now, the biology mistress was also the games mistress and she made you play hockey in the most freezing weather wearing flimsy shorts and a shirt. She was an absolute sadist. So I said, "You know this woman is a sadist. She's obviously made the whole thing up to frighten us. So I wouldn't worry about it." And as a final reassurance I said: "Can you imagine your mum and dad doing that? And what about the Queen?" Well, that clinched it. So we just forgot about it and it never raised its head again until I was 17 and my first boyfriend asked me to do something unspeakable. And it was the same thing! And I couldn't think how he'd heard about it, because he hadn't been to our school. So I explained to him that it was just a malicious story, it wasn't true and nobody did it. Anyway, he thought a bit and then he said, "Well, your friend, does she have a boyfriend?" And she did. So he said, "Will you write to her and ask her if she has ever done this thing that you think is so impossible, and if she has, will you do it?" So I did. And she had!

'So I had it to go through. And it wasn't very pleasant. And after a week, he asked me to do it again! And I said, "Again? I thought you only had to do it once!" '

Today, Kath Thompson of Barrowford complains that modern children know too much. 'My son's eleven and he knows more at his age than I knew at fifteen. It's sad in a way because they have their childhood taken away from them these days with so many unsavoury images and things they don't need to know that are on television. And it's not that they're on after 9 o'clock. All these issues are on before the 9 o'clock watershed and they see them and ask you questions.'

'All the children know everything,' agrees her sister, Diane Rogers. 'We didn't know half the things; like lesbians and gays. I didn't know that.'

John King was 13 or 14 in the early 1970s when he discovered he was gay. 'All the lads at school would be talking about their girlfriends, and I thought, "I haven't got a girlfriend and I don't want a girlfriend." And people kept calling me "puff" so I thought, "There must be something in it." So that's when I decided. I didn't tell my parents until I was 24 because I was an only child and my mum had all these plans for grand-children. I just had to keep it quiet so I didn't disappoint them.'

'As a teenager I was unhappy because I wanted to be like everybody else. I used to hang about on my own. I kept myself to myself. Then I got invited to a party by someone I used to go to school with. And he was there with his friend and I looked at the friend and I thought, "Yes, he looks gay to me." So they asked me and I told them, "Yes." And that was it. My first friend. People noticed a difference in me. I was much happier. I had someone I could talk to and go out with.'

For a young teenage girl going out in the late 1960s in Burnley, Cath Howley was thoroughly ill-prepared for what she met. She was 15 and still at a convent school. But out there were drugs, all-night parties, and the permissive society was just getting into gear. Cath says, the authorities – the nuns at school and parents – seemed to have no idea what was going on, and girls as young as 14 were getting involved. 'My parents didn't stop me going out because they didn't realise it was happening. I'd had no sex education. What I knew came from a book my mum gave me which was very wishy-washy, the girls at school and my boyfriends. They were a great delight!' She recalls her father getting wind that something was amiss. She'd gone down a basement club and was dancing with "the biggest reprobate in the whole place" when he suddenly said, "Gosh, look at that bloke!" And there were these archway doors and there was the shadow of a man in the doorway and he filled the whole doorway. And my boyfriend said, "Bloody hell, someone's in for it!" And I turned round and it was my dad. And he just beckoned with one finger. I can't remember what happened next. I think I've blotted it out from my memory.'

Today, Cath has become that anxious parent – I'm not suggesting that you can fill doorways, Cath, if you should read this – but she's all too aware of the moral dangers which beset young people these days. And the physical dangers as well, especially to younger children. She recalls the nightmare of her own son going missing and her getting the police out recently. It all turned out happily, but she felt justified in her panicky reactions. 'Maybe I did over-react, getting the police out, but there are some very scary people out there today and I don't want my children anywhere near them. She contrasts the situation today with her own childhood in the late 50s:

'We used to set off, and I'd only be six, and we had ponies. And my mum, who was definitely a protective parent, would pack sandwiches and we'd set off to go to Blackpool on our ponies. Nobody batted an eye. And off we'd go. And we'd get maybe to Eddisford Bridge and sit by the river and eat our sandwiches and decide, well, maybe we couldn't get to Blackpool today, we'd better go home and try another day. We came through blissfully unscathed, and it's a pity they can't do that now.'

The kids on the Stoops Estate in Burnley today couldn't even dream of it. They told me:

'We're not allowed to play in the park 'cos there's bad men on all the time ... It's really spoilt round there. There's nowhere to play. There's just bad-habit people round everywhere ... There's loads of rubbish and drug needles and everything.'

Listening to them, you see the face of modern urban childhood and can only weep; weep for the innocence taken from them by the bad world

Kids today on the Stoops estate.

outside. And it's not just drugs and the shabby, squalid landscape that passes for a modern council estate, it's also consumerism. Several of the children I spoke to had been bullied so badly they've had to be taken out of school. And for what? Because they weren't wearing the latest and most fashionable brand names on their clothes.

'Everyone calls you scrubbers if you don't have them. They say you can't afford it and they keep on calling your mum and your dad and your family. They call them druggies and alkies.'

One desperate mother told me, 'We bought some shoes when she was starting high school. They were just plain. And when we got back home all her friends were outside shouting "What shoes have you got? What shoes have you got?" And she wouldn't bring them out. So I had to go and get the catalogue and get her some Kickers. That's how bad it is.'

Poor parents driven to distraction, poor children bullied and dragged, almost before they're out of infancy, into an absurd, competitive world of consumer one-upmanship. No wonder adults look back at those post-war years of poverty and games played under the gaslamps or picnics by a country stream and crave a return to their simplicity and innocence.

Chapter Eight

Getting Older

$\mathcal{A}$s a founder member of the Yoricks, that fifty-something band of armchair anarchists familiar to radio listeners, the theme of getting older should be close to my heart – or furring arteries might be nearer the mark. Having charted time's relentless progress through the glinting of my own skull, scantness of breath and inclination to tear a muscle whilst reaching for my slippers, I can honestly say I was thoroughly at home in many a front room discussing the merits of Philosan or HRT or simply shaking a stubborn stick at a Universe where decay is the only progressive principle and time never moves backwards. But it was particularly interesting to hear people unearth memories of their elderly relatives and see how our attitude to old age has changed throughout the century.

In the past, most elderly relatives seem to have spent their days welded to an armchair or set in monotonous motion in a rocking chair. And to the impressionable eyes of a child, old age could appear rather sinister.

'My mother remembers there being an old, black-clad lady always sitting in a corner of the kitchen and she was not sure who she was,' says Val Thome who is now middle-aged. "She thinks she must have been 'some species of grandmother".'

'It's going back a long way. She was a hideous little old woman dressed in black and she was afraid of her. But that's what they did then: they dressed in black and sat in a corner and watched the life of the household going on around them. This was the great thing about being old in those days, you were totally involved. And when you couldn't get up any more they put you in a bed in the corner. But you didn't miss out on anything. The new babies would be brought in and the pigs and the puppies. You were involved, weren't you? The trouble today is you're not.'

Alice Whittle remembers being terrified by a visit to her Grandma Flynn's in Ormskirk. 'My grandma and granddad lived up a little alleyway and it was a little green door. And my Grandma Flynn, I was terrified of her. Her hair was taken back in a bun at the back of her head. She'd a long,

Elderly tackler in traditional pose.

black coat on. I was terrified. In fact to me, what I'd read in storybooks, she was a witch!'

I don't know whether there are any Grimm's fairy story equivalents amongst grandfathers, but Val Thome found a Shakespearean likeness in hers:

'I remember that when grandma died granddad came to stay with us. He's sold his house and, a bit like King Lear, announced that he was going to spend six months with each of his children. And my mother said it broke his heart when he found out none of them wanted him. When he came to stay at our house he was allowed to use the front room as his personal room, because he was a person who spent his whole life in the front room anyway. My mother tells me that when she was at home the front room belonged to father who lived like a Victorian gentleman and had waxed handlebar moustaches and lived a life of leisure. He sat in the front room and had his meals brought in and had nothing to do with the household whatsoever. They all lived in the back kitchen. But when his wife died he came to live with his family. They were always trying to get rid of him early, making excuses: ringing up the next one on the list and claiming holidays or an illness or redecorating: 'You'll have to take father early.'

Val's grandfather had a particularly objectionable habit. 'Maybe this was why he was put in the front room. He used to make himself little squares of newspaper which he kept in his pocket, and then he would spit copiously into one of these and throw it into the fire. And I remember there being complaints that it sometimes landed on the brasses that my mother had to clean or else missed the fire altogether. And that was what he did most of the time: manufacturing spit balls to throw in the fire.'

Spit balls apart, it's uncanny how stories of grandparents in those days resemble one another. It is as if when you reached a certain antiquity you were expected to behave in a certain way.

The Reverend J. Malcolm Smith of Bury remembers his grandfather coming to live with them at their house in Colne:

'He was a real, almost Victorian figure, a martinet. Smart as paint – he'd been an insurance superintendent – he always used to wear a suit with his diamond solitaire ring, a diamond tie-pin and a waxed moustache with pointed ends which he used religiously to soap every day. When we used to visit him he had his chair, and if you were sitting in grandpa's chair when he walked into the room you got up and got out of it quick. He always seemed to be elderly and he was such a creature of habit. When he came to live with us in Colne after his wife died, he would sit there in the great big leather armchair, which came with him, and he'd sigh, get out one of his cigarettes from a silver cigarette case, tap it three times to shake down the tobacco – none of those tipped ones, because in those days corked-tips were for women or for cissies – and then he'd put on his little gold cigarette holder and he'd light it, then sigh again. And then, at exactly 10 o'clock, you'd get a triple sigh and off he'd go to bed.'

Alice Whittle's Grandma Taylor sat in a rocking chair during her final years and before she became too rheumaticky she used to crochet lace edges to her cotton table cloths and other covers. Which all sounds very grand-motherly. But when it came to her front room, or parlour as Alice prefers to call it, Grandma Taylor became quite a tartar. Everything had to be just so. When Alice used to have to go in to oil the leaves of the aspidistra, she could only go in in her stocking feet and only then after grandma had inspected the bottom of her socks to make sure they were clean. Nothing else in the parlour had to be touched. And if the peg rug in front of the fireplace was as much as an inch out of place, grandma knew. As a 17-

year-old, expected to clean for her grandma, Alice used to find this fastid-iousness quite exasperating, especially when she returned to find her re-dusting the spindle backs of the chairs. But Alice is the first to acknow-ledge that it was only grandma's pride. It was a pride that had kept Lancashire women like her going against the black tide of soot and dirt from the mills, and had kept their heads above water when poverty and destitution threatened to overwhelm them. Such pride dies hard, even when you're frail and have barely strength to pick up a duster in your arthritic hands.

I wondered what Alice's grandma had done for mental stimulation in those days before television. 'She had a valve wireless,' says Alice. 'I can hear it now, whistling and crackling with interference. And she used to read from the big black family Bible nearly every day.' Sometimes she'd ask Alice to sing her her favourite hymn which was 'Rock of Ages', and when she did, 'It was like she was gleaning every word as I sang it.'

Val Thome's Lear-like grandfather would break the monotony of just sitting by taking a small walk every afternoon. 'He had angina and was told to walk extremely slowly. If he came to a pebble in his path, he stopped and hit it out of the way with his walking-stick so that he didn't have to walk round it.' Those Victorians didn't have the greatest Empire in the world by letting things get in their way!

The Reverend Smith's grandfather was cloned from the same stock. His tedious occupation of his armchair was punctuated by regular afternoon 'constitutionals' when weather permitted. With the aid of a silver-topped walking stick he would sally ponderously forth into the local park to exchange his armchair for a park bench where he would sit 'curled up like a little old man.' He was 70.

But we mustn't stereotype old men of his day from a couple of examples. The Reverend Smith's other grandfather was a different glass of Sanatogen altogether:

'I can't help contrasting my other grandfather who sang in a cathedral choir until he was 80. He was involved in sport all his life and played cricket until he was 60. At the age of 70, when the referee didn't turn up, he took the whistle and refereed a football match. And I can remember an occasion when they both came to visit: one grandfather sitting on his park bench while the other, the same age, ran around with us throwing a cricket ball.' He concludes, 'I think a lot was in the mind. Seventy was regarded as being old in those days, whereas nowadays you've got to be in your 80s to be thought of as old.'

Mary Warren, who is 82, reckons people were old at 50 in her grandmother's day. 'And my mother, who lived until she was 80, never looked really young. Admittedly, she hadn't a lot to look young for with four of us to bring up and two world wars in between.'

Her mother would no doubt have been amazed at the energy of her daughter today. Her friend, Alice Lambert, who is in her 90th year outlined her busy schedule for the next day: chiropodist's first thing in the morning followed by the hairdresser's; a cup of tea at her daughter's and then off to the community centre for a session of bingo. 'I'll be out at quarter-past ten and I'll not be in again until quarter-past four. Talk about "Marry me and I promise I won't be at home much," ' she chortles. 'We do very well. There's a lot going for old folk today if you want to do it.'

George Howarth is 95 and his wife Ethel is 89, and they quarrel over whose turn it is to have the car.

'I'm as strong as a lion,' says George, who spent his youth holding pigs down in an abattoir while someone stuck them, and once wrestled a steer in a rodeo in Nelson organised by the cowboy Tex Ritter. 'I'm convinced I'll go on until I'm a 100,' he says. 'I've only had a doctor twice in my

Farmer Jim Cropper, of Deerplay, epitomising the rugged spirit of all the men who have tried to wrest a living out of our hills.

Ron Carter coaxing leaves out of blunt metal.

life.' 'We were put together properly in the first place,' says Ethel. But I left feeling a trifle nervous for them and other road-users. 'I've just got my driving licence extended,' George had told me. 'I'll be 98 when I have to renew it again. I've been done for speeding twice.'

A lifetime spent on our damp Pennine hills has taken its toll on farmer Jim Cropper. 'I've got arthritis with living here, one hip operated on, the other going. It's with walking these hills. A lot of farmers round here suffer the same. It's with going out in all weathers and letting your damp clothes dry on you. Every year I feel a few more joints stiffening up.' And it frustrates him. 'I used to be able to just put my hand on a fencing post and vault over or vault over a wall. You'd spot a sheep a mile away in trouble and you'd set off and run to it and think nothing of it. But you see one now and you think, "It's a long way to walk is that." I have spoilt myself a bit and I've got one of those 4-wheel motorbikes and that gets me about a bit now. But it seems like I'm cheating every time I get on it. I'd rather walk if I could.'

It's sad to hear this. Jim's still a giant figure, with an aura of invincibility about him. You'd think if anyone could resist the onslaught of time it would be him. He epitomises the rugged spirit of all the men who have tried to wrest a living out of our hills, alone with his dog, pitted against a mean and unforgiving Nature. Hewn in the old way, out of gritstone.

And blacksmith Ron Carter, who sadly passed away between the recording and transmission of the radio programmes, is another inspirational figure. I've come away from so many of the people I've spoken to feeling enriched by their warmth and humour and sheer zest for life. No more so than with Ron. After being made redundant in the mill, Ron took up wrought-iron work and became the best in the country at it. Even royalty beat a path to his forge and he made things for Sandringham and Buckingham Palace. I've watched him fashion a tiny vine leaf out of a lump of iron with nothing but a hammer, and it's been fit for a Queen to hang round her neck. Wonderful. He rang as sound and as true as his anvil. And the Hallé Orchestra used to borrow it for their concerts, so there was much good music in him too. It was a rare privilege to know him and he'll be sorely missed. Ron believed passionately in keeping age at bay through exercise. I've seen him at 80 do press-ups like a man of 20 and skip like a child. He knew that bodies will go on working for you well into old age if you keep them busy. If you had shown Ron an armchair, he'd have picked it up and run around the block with it a few times.

For Stanley Graham, steam engine man and historian, growing older gives greater opportunities for mental challenges, and being more bolshie:

'The older I get, the more radical I get. It's a mistake to think that the old, because of their failing powers, tend to become conservative. I've become more radical and vocal. I couldn't give two hoots now what anybody thinks about what I say. I've worked things out and I may be wrong, but I have a point of view and I'll stand on my hind legs and tell people about it. And yes, I don't like the officer class and the playing fields of Eton – as far as I'm concerned, plough 'em up and start growing spuds!'

For some of the middle-aged women I spoke to, growing older in the late twentieth century has its drawbacks. 'It's the physically getting older that I baulk at,' Angela Arnold told me. 'Inside I'm still 16 but the outside lets you down and it's all gravity and the passing of time. It annoys me because we're in a youth culture.' Being divorced, Angela has trouble with men of her own age. 'Men of my age want to go back and look for another 20-odd year-old. They want this silly, fluffy, little hare-brained bimbo to hang on their arm and think they're wonderful. But for me to have a relationship with a 21-year-old boy – I would find it impossible.'

Diane Coulton has one big worry about getting older. 'I'll be a bit upset if my tattoo goes wrinkly.' She has before her the horrid example of her sister: 'She had a bird of paradise on her bum but it's like a golden eagle now!'

And it sounds as if cosmetic surgeons would have a lean time of it in Lancashire. Women like Pat Berry are too philosophical about ageing to go rushing off to spend their hard-earned money on face-lifts and that sort of thing:

'It's inevitable, isn't it? You're born, you get old and you die. There's not a lot you can do about it, is there? Even if I had a lot of money I wouldn't have anything done. I've earned every line I've got and I've enjoyed some of them. But I don't feel any different now than when I was 18, except some mornings when I wake up feeling a hundred and ten.'

For some who have lived through most of the century, so much change has left its mark. 'I'm glad I'm going out and not coming in,' says Doris McWhinney. 'I wouldn't like to be young again, not in this day and age. I think our age was better than it is now. You trusted people and you were happy. You're frightened to death now. You can't answer your door or anything. No, we lived through a better age. I look at these new babies and think, 'What are they going to come to? What will happen to them?' But I suppose they said that about us. They'd think we were coming into a wild world, I suppose.'

The prospect of ending their days in an old people's home is a bleak one for many I spoke to. 'It would break my heart if I had to move from here,' says Mary Greenwood. 'I don't know what I shall do when my son can't look after me. It's very embarrassing for a lady, or a man, to have someone to have to take them to the toilet and that sort of thing, isn't it? So I don't know.'

In the days of Alice Whittle's grandma, this question never arose:

'There were no old people's homes. Oh no, no such thing. People became ill and they were looked after by their family and died in their own home and were laid out by friends and family. There was no such thing as saying, "Well, she's incapable, she can't look after herself, she'll have to go into a home." And that's what is lacking today: family life. It wasn't so much a case of, it's your duty – well, it was your duty but it was a lovely duty. You wanted to do it because you loved them so much even though they were so strict. There were no shades of grey in those days. It was black or white. Right or wrong.'

The problems of getting old in an isolated rural community have already taxed the mind of Les Hardy, who is not yet 60 and lives at Hurst Green in the Ribble Valley.

'The time will come when we will have to consider moving out. I say that because we have the experience of one lady we were very friendly with who, when her husband died and she couldn't drive, had to change from having all the benefits of living in a rural community to becoming almost a prisoner in it. Finally, she had to leave and go to live with her sons in the south. And that's an example that if you become infirm and you haven't got a family close by who can give you support, then it's probably better to consider making a move before it's imposed upon you.'

No amount of forward planning will alter Danny O'Donnell's situation. I met up with him in the Salvation Army hostel in Blackburn. Danny has no possessions apart from one suitcase for his clothes. 'It's not just young people who are homeless but it's middle-aged people like me and even older people. It's all right for younger people who are fit and able, but when you're middle-aged and down-and-out, it's more frightening.'

Alice Whittle recalls that her Granddad Flynn used to take off like a tramp when he became old. The threat of the workhouse hung over the old and the destitute in those days and its shadow never seems to have left the Flynns who had 19 children, though not all of them lived.

'Granddad Flynn would take off for days, walking. When we got a house in Lostock Hall, I remember one particular day seeing this very, very old man and he had a long, torn mac, and he was coming down the road and over his shoulder he had this long twig off a tree and on the end was a red spotted handkerchief. And children were making fun of him. And as I went home this old man – what we'd call an old tramp these days – came nearer and nearer and knocked on our door. And it was my mum's dad, Granddad Flynn.'

But the most vivid recollection of Alice's Granddad Flynn comes from a time when he'd hung up his twig and spotted handkerchief.

'I remember going in this same little house with the green door, and you couldn't move inside for all the families. And there in the corner, stood up in his coffin, was Granddad Flynn. They were having a wake. I remember my mum going right across to him and touching his face. And I can see him now, stood up, starched collar on, suit on and tie, his eyes open, staring, just like you are at me now.'

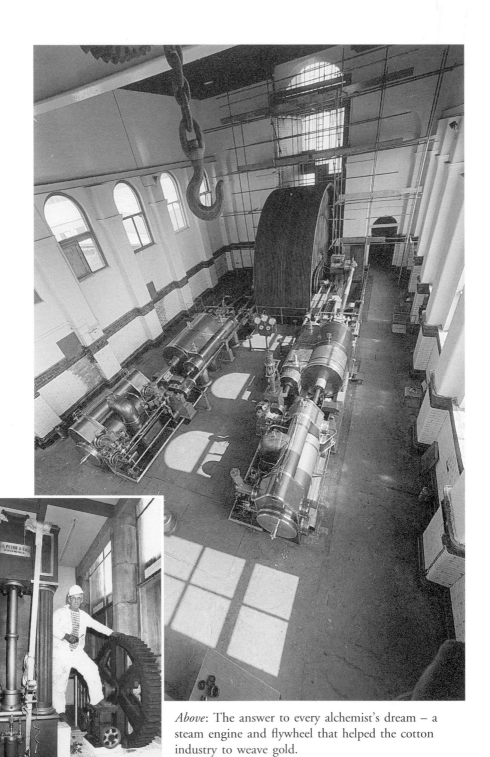

Above: The answer to every alchemist's dream – a
steam engine and flywheel that helped the cotton
industry to weave gold.

Left: Stanley Graham, at home with a mill engine.

Chapter Nine

Technology

STANLEY GRAHAM, who as a younger man minded the steam engine at Bancroft Mill in Barnoldswick, now watches space probes as they happen on the internet. 'If anyone had told me 30 years ago that I'd be doing this I'd have sent for the white van.' The pace of technological advance in the twentieth century leaves most people aghast.

At the beginning of the century the steam engine was king. Every back street end seemed to have its engine house, with a mighty steam engine driving a giant flywheel.

'They were awesome beasts,' says Titus Thornber. 'They were usually housed in almost a palace with great glass windows. And you used to look through these windows and see these huge machines running hour after hour, day after day, year after year. They were a wonderful sight. And then you saw the boiler house with the automatic stokers feeding the coal into the vast boilers.'

I once stood in the engine house at the Ellenroad Spinning Mill in Rochdale which Stanley Graham and a team restored to its former glory in the 1980s, and saw for myself some of the awesomeness of the machinery. Stanley described it to me at the time:

'The engine house is about 100 feet long and 60 feet wide. It's taken up by a massive piece of cast iron, polished brass and blued steel and a flywheel that weighs 85 tons and is 28 feet in diameter. The two cylinders that produce the power deliver it to the flywheel which is further down the engine house; and the flywheel, by means of a system of ropes running up through a huge space in the middle of the mill called the rope race, delivers that power to the shafts which drove the various floors of the mill. If you stood at the top of the rope race it was 200 feet down to the flywheel. It was an absolutely marvellous view. A real cathedral of power.'

But for Stanley Graham the mill engines were more than impressive pieces of engineering. They were a sort of mechanical alchemists' elixir, a means of transmuting the base elements into gold.

A mill boiler, probably weighing about 35 tons, demolishes a house in Burnley in 1907.

'A lot of people get a romantic notion of a steam engine. But it's a very basic thing because by using fire, water and coal (the earth) they produced steam. And they could build steam engines which produced unlimited amounts of power – if you didn't have enough power you built a bigger engine or put another next to it – and out of that combination they made gold. It's the answer to every alchemist's dream. You take air, fire, water and earth and you make gold out of it. It's called the textile industry!'

But the gold spun by the cotton industry was woven at a cost. And I don't just mean the cost in drudgery for the millions of workers in the mills. The technology of steam can be dangerous, as Stanley acknowledges:

'I accept the fact that any sensible man who is dealing with something as elemental and powerful as a Lancashire boiler, with 180lbs per square inch of steam on it or a 3,000 horse power engine, if he doesn't get frightened every now and again there's something wrong. You are dealing with some fairly fearsome technology. If a steam engine is not right and not looked after properly, it can be extremely dangerous.'

Take the Bishop's House disaster in 1945 in Burnley.

'A man was cleaning the engine. He did something he shouldn't have done, which meant that the engine went out of control and started to overspeed. And instead of doing what he should have done, which was to hit the stop motion and stop it, he panicked and ran out of the engine house. The engine overspeeded, got to the point where the flywheel wasn't able to withstand the centrifugal force, the flywheel burst, the engine destroyed itself and in the process of the flywheel bursting it broke through the end wall into the weaving shed and killed a weaver, and at the same time the other bits of the engine flew up, broke the massive beams in the roof and brought down the whole of the sizing department, above which was on top of the engine. At the same time it threw the barring engine – a small engine used to turn the main engine over – out of the main window of the engine house, threw it across the road through the front window of a bedroom and straight on top of the bed. A young lady had just got up to get ready to go to work – the best move she ever made in her life.'

Stanley knew the man whose job it was to sort out all this devastation. 'He said the biggest job was to try and get the barring engine out of the front bedroom of the house. "In the end," he said, "We cleared everything out of the front room, put a lot of waste wood on the floor to act as a cushion, and just sawed through the floorboards around the engine and let it drop into the front room, then got it out through the front of the house." '

Titus Thornber's father was a cotton manufacturer, and as a boy Titus was able to wander wherever he pleased in the mill. He witnessed the

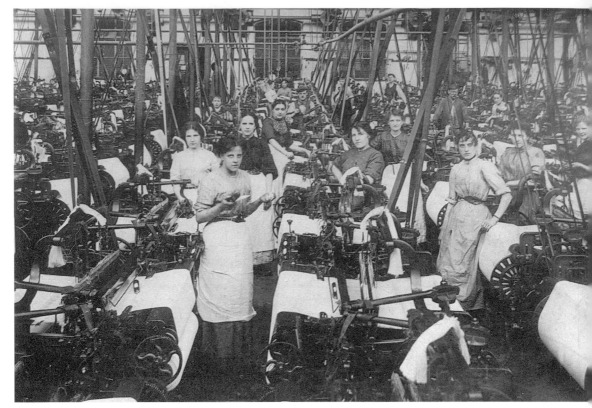

How did the women escape injury working in such confined conditions?

pandemonium of the weaving shed, with its 'mass of whirring machinery', particularly the belts which came down from the shafting in the roof and drove the looms.

'The most terrible accidents were where men's clothing was caught. The whole of the mill was a mass of shafting and leather belts, admittedly guarded to a certain extent. But some of the mechanics had to climb up ladders and attend to things and if their clothing was caught by a leather belt they were dragged round the shafting. Oh, it was a terrible death! There was the whole of the power of the steam engine behind it and no one could stop it quickly enough to save you.'

Muriel Blenkinsop remembers what happend to her Uncle Jim:

'He was a grand chap. He worked at the Great Leaver Spinning Company in Bolton. He went out to work one morning at about twenty-five to eight and before 8 o'clock he was dead. He worked in the engine room. At that time in the mill they wore what they called "slops". They were short, blue denim jackets, and they wore a bib-and-brace overall underneath. And in the engine room the ropes used to go through from one floor to another, and he happened to be standing near it and his jacket caught. And he was swung round the shafting. It pulled him up and he hit his head on the ceiling and then fell to the floor dead.'

Like all boys of that era, Titus Thornber used to love to watch the steam locomotives.

'A steam locomotive was like a huge, panting beast, especially when, for example, it was drawing away from Euston or St Pancras Station in London with 16 or 17 carriages behind on a 400-mile run to Edinburgh. It was a moving sight and sound. And then, where we lived, we were on the only low-level rail pass between Lancashire and Yorkshire and there were massive coal trains going through the valley, with the huge engines panting and puffing away to drag a thousand tons of coal up to the summit of the pass. They were the most stirring sights and sounds.'

I can vouch for this. Earlier this year I stood at the line side on the same stretch of track through the Cliviger Valley making a recording for the radio series. A steam preservation society had organised an excursion, and to witness two locomotives fully loaded charging up the gradient towards Windy Bridge, the Pennine watershed where the two River Calders start their different journeys, was indeed a stirring sight. Billowing clouds of black smoke spewed from their funnels and the roar of the engines and shriek of their whistles echoed off the primal escarpments of the Cliviger Gorge. Everything I'd heard about the raw, elemental force of steam power coalesced in that moment into an unforgettable experience.

Stanley Graham puts his finger on what it is about the old mechanical technology which makes it so visually impressive:

'There's one thing about steam engines and steam locomotives – their guts are hung out and you can see how they work. And if you can actually see how they're working, that's exciting. Would my enthusiasm ever have been as great about an electric motor that just sits there and buzzes? I don't think so. I've yet to hear of an electric motor preservation society.'

It's an interesting point, and I wonder if it begins to explain that species of Lancashire man, now well into middle-age and older; a generation of tinkerers and fettlers who you'll find today with a spanner in their hands on the Worth Valley Railway, a smear of oil and a smile across their happy faces, or tucked away in a shed at the bottom of a backyard coaxing the swarf off a piece of metal on a lathe as they restore something or other.

Is it something about the urban landscape they grew up in, either before or just after the war, surrounded by steam trains chugging across viaducts, giant pistons glinting from every engine house? Did it sow the seeds of a lifetime's passion for all such things mechanical. An intimate rapport?

If it's washing, it must be Monday.

Stanley Graham reckons it might have done. He recalls living in Stockport as a child: 'The whole of the middle of the town was full of industry. It wasn't like it is now. They didn't try to zone industry. Factories were where they'd grown up, not tucked away on industrial estates. For instance, if you went shopping, there was a foundry on the main shopping street. And my mother used to stop so that I could watch them pouring metal into the moulds. And as kids, we wanted to be in there. In fact, many a time, when we came out of school, instead of going home we'd go down to the locomotive shed. And we could walk round and they'd give us a ride on the loco to the coaling shute. I actually once drove a loco: pulled the lever, made it start and stopped it. Can you imagine that happening nowadays?'

On the domestic front, technology took a long time before it liberated the working mum from the drudgery of housework.

'My mother used to spend all day Monday down the cellar and it was all steam down there,' recalls Muriel Blenkinsop. Boiling water in set pans or filling dolly tubs. Pounding possers. Dragging out ponderous mangles and winding through soggy sheets. It sounds a Herculean task compared to today's push-button doddle.

'It was absolutely awful,' says Joan Driver. 'We had an old gas boiler and you used to have to light it underneath with a taper. You turned on the gas, stuck the taper in and backed-off quick. "Boom!" '

Then technology arrived and suspicion came with it. 'My mother got a Bendix washer, and, I'm telling you, she had it twelve months before she would use it. She still had the old boiler.'

If Monday was washing day and you managed to survive life amongst the forest of drying clothes hanging from the overhead rack and the clothes maiden round the fire, Tuesday dawned to a pile of ironing. Agnes Cross remembers having a box iron:

'It had a little lid and you lifted this lid up and it had heaters inside to fit it; and you heated them up in the fire and they had a hole in the top where you put your poker through to lift them out of the fire and into the iron. You'd to keep a good fire to heat them up because they needed to be red hot. And you had two or three heaters in the fire at once because they didn't stay hot in the iron and you'd to keep changing them all the time you were ironing. Some had flat irons that you put against the stove chimney to heat them up and some had charcoal irons; and there were gas irons too.'

Mary Warren remembers buying a neighbour's electric iron and vacuum cleaner off her because the neighbour had moved into a house that only had gas. 'Well, I were the bees knees then. Folk were borrowing my vacuum because they'd never been near one before. And my iron. I didn't know whether it was mine or the woman's next door. I used to have to go and get it back when I wanted to use it. This was in 1942 or 1943. The war was on.

Born at the beginning of the First World War, there were no such things as wireless sets when Titus Thornber was a boy. 'The only home entertainment was playing games such as snakes-and-ladders and ludo. There was no institutionalised palliative for the people like the BBC.' (Note that phrase, BBC bosses!) 'I remember so clearly how it burst upon us this sudden realisation that a programme could be transmitted into your very living-room. People went for it in a really big way. They wanted the first wireless set so badly they were prepared to make their own, and a huge industry developed. You bought a sheet of ebonite and drilled holes in it, and you had terminals and learnt how to solder with a copper soldering

iron stuck in the fire. And you learnt about things like Fluxite and tinning
the wire with solder, winding coils and painting them with shellac. In every
household the men were doing this and making their own wirelesses. To
begin with, you could only listen with headphones and people sat round
all listening and grinning at one another.'

But Titus, as befits his wonderful old-fashioned name, is convinced that
the radio revolution was a 'retrograde' step. 'When people made their own
entertainment it was developing their capabilities and discovering new
talents. Just sitting there listening to something, you're not discovering
anything, are you?'

Jack Nicholls, brought up in the Rossendale Valley after the war, is now
the Bishop of Sheffield. He's convinced that the advent of television has
had a similarly stunting effect, this time on our social development. He
thinks that as people got their televisions they 'stopped participating in
life.' He recalls the ritual of watching TV in the early 1950s:

'People went to the house of a member of the family who had a television
and they closed the curtains, and if you were posh you had a magnifying
glass in front of the television that made the screen look bigger.'

Roger Frost remembers kids from the whole neighbourhood coming to
his house. 'We had the first television in Harle Syke on the left-hand side
of Burnley Road. We had quite a big front room and sometimes there'd
be twenty or more children in there watching it. I think it was a nine-inch
screen with a big magnifier in front of it which I once knocked over and
it broke. It was full of liquid that stained all the carpet.'

Roger's father was a great believer in new technology. Not only did they
have the first television in the neighbourhood, but they had the first
microwave, a very primitive affair, according to Roger. And there was always
an up-to-date washing-machine to ease the labour of servicing a large family.
But even Mr Frost's enthusiasm for new-fangled things didn't blind him
to the negative effects of technological progress:

'My father always said that the introduction of the automatic washer
would contribute to the breakdown of the community, because people
would no longer have to put their washing out on the line and meet each
other every washing day. To talk over the backyard gate was one of the
great institutions of yesterday.'

You could argue that today the telephone has become a universal backyard
gate. But Barbara Robinson of Blackpool remembers that it was not so
long ago that when you were ordering something from a shop, the salesman
would enquire politely, 'Do you have a phone?' and the answer was
invariably, 'No.' These days they automatically assume that you will have

Progress has bypassed this old mill, with the workers' houses built up to the mill wall and the old engine house to the right. Slater Terrace, Burnley, 1999.

one. My favourite story of technological naivety concerns the telephone and came from Ben Barnes, a road haulier from Rossendale.

It was wartime and Ben broke an axle shaft on his lorry near Lichfield. He could see some telephone wires going to a farmhouse so he followed them and asked to use the phone to summon assistance from back home. The farmer was a bit apprehensive about his phone reaching as far as Rawtenstall.

'Ee,' he said, 'I don't think it'll go that far.' 'Well,' I said, 'it should do. Can I try?' So when I'd got through to my dad the farmer said, 'Hang on a minute, just let me have a word with him.' And when my dad told him he was speaking from 18 miles north of Manchester, the farmer was astonished and said, 'Ee, can I ring you again?' He'd probably be telling everyone in the auction next day, 'Ee, I spoke to a bloke the other side of Manchester last night!'

A glimpse of today's computerised technology would have rendered any old-fashioned telephone user speechless and reduced them to semaphore.

It's an interesting transformation to observe that with the demise of textiles, the aerospace industry has become one of Lancashire's most prominent employers. Many old mills that once housed steam engines and resounded to the clatter of looms have now been modernised to make room for lathes and complicated modern machinery for the manufacture of aircraft parts.

Today's lathes are largely noiseless. Run by computer and housed inside special chambers, they are so advanced that even their operators can hardly take in the speed of progress. Forsaking overalls for golf shirts and sweaters bearing the firm's logo, the engineers no longer get their hands dirty or scratched in the spray of oil and water and metal fragments but stand at a computer screen full of unfurling data. Today there's nothing to stop a million-pound machine being run by a man 100 miles away with a lap-top computer.

When I visited a converted cotton mill in Foulridge, home of the hi-tech Weston Electrics, I spoke to a group of workers who told me:

'I've seen so many changes over the last 28 years since I started and I just can't comprehend in my own mind where we're going to be in another 28 years. It's mind-boggling ... What you say is right, you always look at the future with a certain amount of trepidation, especially when we've reached the situation where if you buy the most brand new up-to-date PC it's been superseded within three months. When we first started working on the first computerised machines the difference between that and the latest machine that we installed last week – well, it makes the old one look like a steam engine.'

But it takes a lot more than a computer to impress Titus Thornber:

'A computer can only turn out what the brain of man has put into it. It cannot supersede man's brain or workmanship. So I'm not overawed at all by computers. I'm staggered at the incredible number of functions that a miniature circuit can perform these days and the speed with which it can do it. They defy understanding. But they don't impress me anywhere near as much as a huge steam railway engine pulling 800 tons of coal up the Cliviger Valley.'

Perhaps our machines say more about the era in which they are born than we think. And the steam engine came from an age which still had some poetry in its soul.

≈ *Chapter Ten* ≈

Eating and Drinking

THE STORY OF FOOD over the century seems to be the story of a loss of control over what we eat. In the period up to the Second World War the housewife often baked her own bread and cakes. In the farming communities they salted their own hams, boiled pigs' heads to make brawn, made black puddings, and people grew and ate their own vegetables from their own plots and allotments. So while refrigeration and preservatives may have broadened our diet beyond recognition and our awareness of more healthy eating has outlawed large fat intakes, our reliance on factory foods has left many of us with an almost romantic desire for the days of wholesome organic foodstuffs and baking just like grandma used to do. So it's good to revel in the memories of home-produced food.

Emma Edge was born in 1898 and brought up on a farm in Bacup. She remembers baking day on a Thursday:

'My mother would have the table full of bread, plain teacakes, currant teacakes – it was absolutely ram, jam full. And on Friday morning, for our breakfast we'd have a plain muffin, and if we'd killed a pig and had some bacon, we'd have it put into t' dip, never mind t' bacon. Ooh, and do you know, it were good!'

It was the same in Edgar Wormwell's house in Kelbrook near Earby. 'I used to like her oven-bottom cakes and the smell of new bread when she'd been baking. Oh, it was different altogether!' But the effort involved didn't escape the notice of the young Edgar:

'It looked like it were hard to me. She'd have a big baking bowl and her sleeves rolled up and she'd be kneeding this dough, and I've seen the sweat running down her face. But it used to smell lovely!'

A flour bag had to be taken to the Co-op before baking could begin. 'It was like a pillow-case,' says Muriel Blenkinsop. 'You'd go to the Co-op and you'd want a half-a-dozen of flour and two ounces of barm. You'd go to the flour boy, who was the errand boy as well. They didn't like to sell you the flour in bags, though they did have it already packed, but I don't think

A proudly restored fire range. The left-hand bottom panel contained the boiler from which bathwater was drawn. Top right was the bread oven.

they liked the job, so you'd hold out your flour bag while he got it out of a bin and put it in and weighed it. And then you took a piece of string and tied it around the top of your bag. And if you'd a lot to carry, you'd have a basket in either hand and the flour bag on top of your head to walk home.'

'My mum always made an Eccles cake for my dad,' recalls Edgar Wormwell. 'He had one every teatime to finish off his meal. And he used to warm it in front of the fire. He used to slot it between the bars at the front of the fire and you could hear the fat in it sizzling. But it used to keep dropping out onto what we used to call the tidy Betty. Anyway, I'd just started work at Dotcliffe Mill and I made him a little gadget that slotted into this bar with two sharp points on and he could rest his sad cake on it. It never dropped down again.'

Fat intake in those days sounds to have been prodigious. 'The Eccles cakes were made with suet,' says Edgar. 'I suppose they had to have a lot of fat in those days to keep 'em warm when they were working out of doors. I've heard him say that my grandfather, when they set off to work in the morning, the last thing he did was to go into the kitchen and he'd empty all the bacon fat into a pint pot and drink it.'

Just to hear a story like that is enough to give a modern heart surgeon a thrombosis. But John Parkinson tells me that bacon was the staple diet of the working man, good fatty bacon.

'We used to trade with the farmers on the canal boats. We'd sell him a bag of coal and he'd give you a piece of bacon. You'd take this bacon, all white and lovely, and you'd put it in the frying pan. And as soon as you'd cooked the bacon, before you put eggs in the pan or anything' (He never bought any eggs but knew where hens were laying or waterhens or ducks) 'you'd drain the fat into a cup. The salt deposits in the bottom was your dripping and the working man lived off that. They lived off what they used to call 'browis': you buttered bread with dripping and put it in a cup and poured hot water on it and ate it, the same idea as pobs. That was your early morning breakfast.'

When Emma Edge's father killed a pig, nothing got wasted. 'We'd have all the offal: the liver, kidneys, heart, and my mother would get a bit of shin beef and an onion and put that with it, and she'd make "black dish". Ooh and it were good! She'd cook it in a big brown dish which held about seven pounds and she'd cook it in the oven. And it would last us for three or four days would that, and Ee, it were good!'

The day a pig was killed was always a big day on the farm. Evelyn Holt-Horsfall never dared watch. She used to see the pig being carried into one of the buildings with its legs tied together and a pole passed through.

Then she used to hear the terrible squeals. Ruth Collinson kept her distance, too. 'You'd see them walk the pig from the pig-house to the dairy and then you'd hear all this noise and the next thing you knew, the door opened and all this steam came out. They'd got the pig and they'd fastened it to a ring in the wall and cut its throat and let all the blood run into a bucket. And someone had to be there to stir it to make sure it didn't thicken because mum would make black puddings. And the hot water had gone from the house to pour onto the pig to scrape the hairs off. And whoever was there stirring the blood always got splashed. What she actually did to make the black puddings was to use this metal dish which she lined with something from the pig she used to call the 'net curtains' which had little slivers of fat through it. And she'd cut the fat up and put the seasoning in and when it had been cooked you could cut it into slices. She made beautiful black puddings. Today they don't taste like mother used to make them. They were lovely.'

The rest of the pig would be cut up and salted from blocks of crushed salt. 'Dad would salt the meat and it would be laid on the big stone slabs in the pantries. And there were holes in the stone slabs for any surplus brine to drain through. And then he'd leave them for so many weeks before bringing them up into the kitchen and rolling them and stringing them. And he would take his leather belt off to help him roll the bacon tighter. Then it would be hung in the pantry.'

On Emma Edge's farm they used to hang the sides of bacon up on a beam in the kitchen. 'And my mother used to make Christmas puddings and hang them there, too, in rags. In fact, I knew a fellow who lived next door who used to bury his in the ground. He said it kept 'em better.'

Donald Barker remembers having to scrape the mildew off his mother's Christmas puddings. 'You never thought owt about it and they were lovely and sweet inside.'

Friday night was broth night at Colin Cooke's dad's pub, The Four Alls in Higham.

'We used to give free broth in winter time. We used a big iron pan that we used to wash the bedding in on a Monday. And it were broth, Ooh! They used to say, broth's not reet until t'spoon stands up in it. This were sheep's head broth with dumplings, real suet dumplings. And we used to prick them and fill them with pepper. They'd sup some ale when they'd had some of those dumplings. They'd blow your head off!'

For all the dripping and suet consumed, Ron Carter doesn't remember there being a lot of obesity. 'Jobs then used to use up a lot of energy and we didn't have a lot of food. There was no overeating like there is today.'

Ron remembers having Lancashire hot pot, meat and potato pie and cow heel and the cheaper cuts of meat. 'We were poor. In fact, mother used to send me to the butcher for a sheep's head for sixpence and that was our weekend joint. And she'd cook it and make it beautiful. She'd wrap the brains in a cloth and that was a delicacy with a bit of butter. And she'd make a broth with the sheep's head with barley.'

Donald Barker's neighbour was Mrs Gregory who lived in Water Fold. She had four sons and her husband to feed and they all worked in the pit:

'She had a big cast-iron cooking pot on the open fire and in the winter it was never taken off for three months. There was a rabbit put in or a lump of meat. There were bones put in or a pigeon. And they had it every time they came home from the pit. There was always something going into that pot. Some of the gravy from it would have knocked you over, it was that strong. Some of the bones were in that long they'd melt away, and every now and again they'd get a cloth and seive it and throw the bones away. I'll allus remember that pot.'

Hettie Cunliffe's dad was a good cook – they'd taught him in the army in the First World War when he was injured and could no longer fight. The only trouble was, he was too extravagant. 'I'll cook the dinner this Sunday,' her mother used to tell him, 'We're hard-up this week.'

'The trouble was, if he cooked a shoulder of lamb it ended up half the size. He'd take all the runners out of the oven and put the hook in the top and hang it there with a full tin of potatoes underneath. Well, my mother made it do two meals by cooking it in a pot so it didn't shrink. If he made a custard he'd use a roasting tin and use about six eggs,' says Hettie, still managing to sound scandalised to this day.

When a cow had calved on the farm, Hilda Parkinson's mum used to make a 'beast' pudding out of the first milk from the cow. 'It made a lovely thick custard.' As a child Hilda doesn't remember anything like cereals for breakfast, only bread and milk or 'pobs'.

Life in Arthur English's household in Barrowford was dominated by the mill, where all the family worked. His parents took their breakfast at their looms and Arthur used to come in to join them before he went to school.

'It was usually a banana, a currant teacake with jam on it and a pot of tea. Monday's dinner was always what his mother had prepared on a Sunday night, usually a meat and potato pie or a hot pot with slices of potato on the top that had gone nice and crisp. 'Arthur had to rush home from school and heat it up ready for his parents coming home from the mill. On Tuesday, Wednesday and Thursday his grandma made the dinners – hot pot, meat and potato pie – Arthur admits the meals didn't vary very much

– and he'd to stand at the end of May Street where his grandma lived, and as soon as he saw his parents coming along Maud Street he had to put the dishes in a basket and carry them home. Friday's dinner was always fish and chips, and he'd to stand in the queue and hadn't to get them until he saw his parents going home so they could all have them hot with bread and butter and a cup of tea.

Fish and chips was an ideal meal for busy weavers. Muriel Blenkinsop remembers being sent for them with a basin with a piece of paper over it, an early form of take-away. She used to get mushy peas with her fish and chips. When she moved from Lancashire to Yorkshire she was six months before she could face fish and chips. 'I couldn't bear the smell of them because they used dripping in Yorkshire whereas we always used pure lard in Bolton.' Alice Greenwood's parents had a fish and chip shop in Bury and she can remember when they changed to frying in oil. 'We used to notice the difference. People used to say, "Hm, these are good." But my father would never tell them it was oil because he reckoned they wouldn't have wanted it if they had known. But they were much better.'

You wonder, with all this talk of fat and frying, whether anybody ever bothered with vegetables. Arthur English remembers salads with cold meat being regularly served up for tea. 'We had a garden and grew our own tomatoes and lettuce and scally onions and things.' It was a co-operative effort amongst the gardeners of the Rossendale Valley around Water. Donald Barker's father would swap some of his favourite golden ball turnips which he'd grown for someone else's King Edward potatoes. No money ever changed hands and he can't remember them ever buying vegetables in summer time.

One particularly unexpected treat for the young Donald was when he and his chums begged a wooden barrel from the greengrocer's to play with. They found it had a false bottom containing eight bunches of lovely green grapes. 'I didn't go to school for two days after eating so many grapes.'

Sunday tea was generally the time for something more exotic. Alice Whittle is ashamed to admit that she only looked forward to a preacher from chapel coming to tea for one reason:

'It sounds mercenary and disgusting this, but it's the truth. I always knew when a preacher was coming for his tea because we'd have salmon. John West's salmon! And also my mum would make a pineapple trifle. Imagine! John West's salmon and this pineapple trifle with whipped cream on. Ooh!'

Rather than having associations of gastronomic superiority like they have today, oysters were very popular with ordinary people and they were cheap and plentiful. Tom Kennedy's father kept an oyster bar in Blackburn for forty years after the First World War. 'People would come in,' says Tom, 'feeling a bit unwell, usually self-inflicted wounds from beer the night before, and have half-a-dozen oysters to put them right. A complete fallacy, of course. It didn't do anything to you except make you feel good, you know?'

In the 1920s, Ethel Howarth's father kept hens, at a time when eating chicken was a luxury. They thought nothing of having chicken at the weekend. 'Everyone thought we were right posh. But we were fed up of it. But then my mother bought a little goat and it used to run around in the house like a pet dog. Then suddenly it disappeared and we found we'd eaten it. That must have been why my mother bought it. But we all wept gallons of tears because we'd eaten this goat.'

'There wasn't as much exotic food around as there is today,' says Ken Hartley, who began work for a greengrocer in Nelson before the war. But it seems that people were more discerning about what they bought.

'I mean, today you go to a supermarket and you look at the produce, the potatoes, say, and I wouldn't give them houseroom. They wouldn't have been sold in the old days because of their poor quality: there's cuts on them and they've been bashed. They'd have been straight back onto the grower in the old days. And people wouldn't buy them, either. They couldn't afford to be throwing stuff away like they are these days, and they'd bring it back to the shop and complain. They were more discriminating.'

Colin Cooke, who was a butcher from the age of 14 until he retired, has a similar gripe about today's meat:

'Do you know why meat's lost its flavour? They're spray and fertilizer mad. When we used to go down a field there'd be clover and all sorts of flowers, and that's where the meat got its flavour. Ee, the beef used to be good! And they used to bring them in and let them settle before they killed them. But now they're all tensed up with being carted about and things and the meat never sets right. And they wash it all down with pressure pipes. Well, a certain amount of water goes into the meat and again it doesn't set right. We used to wipe them with a rag. But they won't be told, all these experts these days. They think they know it all.'

But the most passionate indictment of modern methods of food production comes from Chris Johnson, an organic food specialist who runs the Village Restaurant in Ramsbottom. He traces the time when food lost its innocence, and started to lose its taste, to the last war. The use of fertilizers and other chemicals had helped to boost food production, and after the war the Attlee Government did everything in its power to encourage farmers and agricultural suppliers to make farming more industrial and hence productive.

'Scientists began to realise that by changing things, by cross-breeding and supplying fertilizers and poisons, they could greatly increase the yield of food. Now we are crossing species which are entirely unnatural. Put the anti-freeze genes from an Arctic flounder into a strawberry and you can refrigerate it much more to extend its supermarket shelf-life. By transgenic farming so many things are being put at risk purely in the interest of profit.'

And the taste? Chris is convinced that organically grown food and animals reared in the old-fashioned way can still be found here in Lancashire:

'I think that proper bacon made out of old-fashioned fatty pigs where you've got at least fifty-per cent fat, put in the frying pan and sizzled away so that the fat is crisp and gold; some bread made from organic flour put into the bacon fat to make glorious golden fried bread – wonderful!'

And if that begins to sound like what Emma Edge was tucking into 90 years ago, don't be surprised. It is. It seems there's no such thing as twentieth-century progress as far as good food is concerned. So stick that in your Big Mac and eat it!

Chapter Eleven

Money

I THINK 'Lack of Money' would have been a more appropriate title for this chapter in order to capture the almost universal experience of Lancashire folk throughout the best part of this century. Tales of conspicuous wealth were as rare as stories of brainy tacklers, and the one person I spoke to who had dragged himself up by his clog laces until he finally owned a Rolls-Royce was too sheepish to talk much about it. I think it's safe to say we don't much care for people who brag about their wealth and if we ourselves have anything, we usually keep quiet about it. They used to say that Sydney Silverman, who was the Labour MP for Nelson and Colne when I was a lad, would leave his Rolls-Royce parked outside the borough boundary and come in on the bus. I don't know whether this is true, but if it is, he showed good sense. They might call it social envy these days, but in the old days it was lack of money which united us. Poverty was a tribal mark, and if you had money you didn't really belong: you inhabited a different world, like the mill-owners up on the hill where the air was sweet and soot-free and life and the sun smiled on you.

So it's poverty which is the theme of this chapter, the sort that exposed itself in every threadbare detail of David Palmer's home life in Barnoldswick back in the 1940s.

'Every Sunday night my mother used to put a fresh piece of cardboard in the bottom of my shoes to cover the holes, and my sister's too. There were nowt else.'

George Andrews goes back further, to the hungry 30s in Waterside in Colne:

'The out-of-work used to stand on the bridge, and to me they looked really old fellas. They were only in their late 30s, but they looked old and shabby with patches on their clothes and their shoes worn down. They looked old but they weren't. It were the conditions they lived in, weren't it?'

And back another decade to Burnley after the First World War, when Titus Thornber was a boy and had to walk through the slums to get into

A nice bit of self-parody from the 1920s.

Home not-so-sweet home with slopstone, mangle and iron range.

the town centre: back-to-back houses thrown up at the beginning of the cotton era where the poverty was appalling and the gutters ran with human excrement. We can only imagine what conditions must have been like inside these houses. But the outsides of the landings which George Andrews witnessed in Waterside gives a good idea:

'They were hovels. A landing came out and there were pillars, with houses underneath that went into the hillside. The back walls must have been terribly damp, and they were dismal because no light got in because of the landings. When you looked in they looked dark. They must have been terrible to live in.'

When Lizzie Hartley's father drove her from his door because she was courting her injured war-hero, whom her father cruelly called 'that peg-leg', she had to stay with her cousin Thyra for 6 months:

'They only had a one-up and one-down and there were 5 of them, three of them little children. "I'll make room," she said. "You're going to sleep in this room with us and I'll put mats down and a pillow, and I have a big maiden we'll put round with a red quilt over the top".'

Conditions in David Palmer's home were no better 25 years later. 'We had a stone floor, a peg rug and a black-lead grate. We'd a kitchen with a slopstone in it and that was it. We were destitute.'

Hettie Cunliffe, a life-long Salvationist now in her 90th year, is convinced God answered their prayers when her father went away to the First World War and they were left penniless, though I think even she might admit that He moves in mysterious ways:

'It would be a week or so after my father had gone to the war, my mother wasn't working because she was pregnant, and apart from that she'd fallen and hurt two ribs. And she had no money for six weeks. But I can remember this morning – I'd be about six-and-a-half – and we had some bread and jam and porridge for our breakfast and afterwards my mother said 'I don't know what I'm going to do about your dinner, I have nothing at all.' And before I went off to school, she got down on the hearth and she put her arms round me and my brother and I can remember her praying and asking God to help her to get some food for our dinner.'

'Anyway, I went to school and when I came home for my dinner the table was set and me and my brother had a boiled egg each. And I said, "I thought you said we'd no dinner?" And she said, "Yes, but we prayed, didn't we?"'

'What had happened was, just after I'd gone to school my mother heard such a commotion in the street. And there were two old ladies who lived opposite and one of them was at her door screaming and carrying on. Well, apparently her sister was dead in her chair. Anyway, my mother calmed her down, sent for the doctor, and stopped to help wash her and lay her out. And the woman was so grateful to her she gave her a two shilling piece. So she bought two eggs, a bit of margarine and a loaf of bread, and my mother had a bit of jam in the house, so she had bread and jam and we had an egg apiece.'

The dismal living conditions in the pre-war milltowns of Lancashire, and the widespread poverty meant that suicides were all-too common. Lynn Millard was a Burnley policeman and one of the saddest cases he was ever called to was in Mitre Place, still a rather doleful quarter of the town if you wander amongst the carcasses of the old mills on the canal side.

'When I did get there, the man was dead. It was a little one-room he lived in, and I was searching round for a suicide note when I found a little club book for a tallyman – where people could get stuff in advance and pay it off every week. And he had a little card for a blanket which he was paying off at sixpence a week.'

Sometimes it's important to remember that these stories of poverty are told by elderly people who are speaking about what happened to them as children, and we all know how good parents will shield their children from the worst experiences. It is often the little details that go unheeded by the child at the time which in later life they recognise to be symptoms of the family's terrible plight. But Ron Carter must have had a good idea how bad things were for his mother in Ashton-under-Lyne during the Depression:

'All the children in those days walked with the scholars on Whit Monday, and they had banners. And I remember I could never go. Mum used to say, 'Don't bother going this year, leave it till next.' And I realize now that it was because I'd no clothes to wear. And one year, I'll never forget it, my mother said, 'You're walking with the scholars this year.' I'd probably be 10 or 11. And she'd got me this suit, and she was paying it off at sixpence a week. And it was a cheap thing. I suppose if it had got rained on it would shrivel up. And I put this suit on, little short pants, and my mates came and said, 'We're going to Fiddler's pit, which was full of water on Ashton Moss. And we were playing and these two lads came along and one of them fell in the pit. And I tried to reach to get him out and he went further in. So I went a bit closer and he was fighting. He must have been swallowing water. He was going under. So I went further in and he was still fighting me. I thought, 'He's going to drown, is this lad! 'So I pushed off. I could swim. And I butted him to the edge, and his brother got him and he was there vomiting. But I was thinking about me suit. And I tried to rub it down with grass. They were all rubbing me down,

Ron Carter. Ron Carter never did tell how he saved a lad's life.

were these lads. Anyway, I got home and I opened the door to go in, and my mother took one look at me and gave me one swipe. Bang! And I knew I deserved every bit of it. And I never did tell her about saving this lad's life. The suit was far more important than what happened.'

A hundred lectures from historians and sociologists about the extent and causes of poverty cannot for me compare with that one graphic anecdote from Ron Carter. It is stuff like this that makes oral history so arresting and worthwhile. I only hope the scholars of the future who come to listen to these interviews when they're lodged in the British Library for posterity will be as moved as I was to hear it and will accord it the importance it deserves.

Just as it was important to keep your front doorstep donkey-stoned and your window-sills clean as a gesture of pride and civilised defiance against all the grime from the mills, so it was important that your children were turned out well for Sunday school and on walking days, however poor you were. Hilda Parkinson remembers always having new clothes for walking days. 'My mum always made sure we were dressed nice for that day. We had bonnets on and a basket full of flowers. She always had us nice for that. But we'd no money. For her husband John's family, the first priority was always food:

'More or less every penny that we had was for food and the horses. The horses were part of the job for a canal boatman. My parents would manage a night out at the pictures in Preston and my dad liked a pint or two. Liking your ale was part and parcel of being a boatman. In fact, I know one or two firms that I've worked for whose first question before they employed you was, 'Are you a tea-totaller?' And if you were, there was no way you could get a job. They didn't like them sort of morose people that wouldn't have a drink. They preferred to employ drinkers, the idea being that if they're spending their money on food and all the essentials and having a pint or two, at each pay day they'd end up near enough skint. So you'd give 'em more money and they'd set to and work again. You could trust a man like that because there was the impetus to work.'

So far as I know, this is a completely novel economic theory that I bet you'll never find in any textbook. What's more, I believe it. It will not please the anti-drinking lobby, but I love your phrase 'a morose tea-totaller', John. In fact, I'll drink to it.

Like farmers, canal men always had to have a bit of money put aside to replace an animal. 'It was kept under the bed or in a tin box,' says John Parkinson. 'It wasn't put into a bank. One of the richest places I ever came to was Nelson. There were more penny banks in Nelson than I've seen anywhere. These cotton weavers would keep crying poverty, but they must have had some money somewhere.'

Arthur English, being from Nelson, would probably deny this. He points to Trawden, near Colne, as the home of the canniest.

'Now Trawden is a funny place. It's allus been said they owned their own house and the one next door. My wife's granddad was from Trawden and he had a thousand poultry, ran four looms at the mill and when they had a week off he'd go helping with the haymaking at the farm at the end of the lane.' And then he pauses, and I think he's going to tell me just how rich he was. But prudence prevails. Instead, all he would say was, 'It was not how much you had, it was how much you could leave.'

When Lizzie Hartley had finished sleeping on the floor at her cousin Thyra's, she married her Robert. She must have thought she'd landed on her feet. Before they moved into the cottage next door, Robert told her: 'I'll tell you what to do. In the morning ask the boss if he'll let you out for an hour and go down to Dean and Hirst's and have a bedroom suite made and I'll pay for it.' 'There was the wardrobe, a dressing table, a pair of drawers and the bed, all solid oak and dove-tailed. Guess how much? £19. And it were lovely.'

Ruth Monaghan, who lived in Fleetwood, was not so lucky, and this was 25 years later. 'When we got married in 1948, we bought everything second-hand. We gave £25 for a three-piece bedroom suite, and it was walnut and I'm still using it today.'

In those days, people rarely went into debt. 'That was a shameful thing,' says Joan Driver. 'My mother used to say, 'You sit on orange boxes if you can't afford chairs, until you can afford them.' This has led her to a modern suspicion of plastic money. Joan always holds her Auntie Lily from Blackpool up as a model of financial prudence. Auntie Lily didn't believe in banks or cheques and always carried her money with her. 'She'd had a mastectomy and she always kept her money in her bra.'

For David Palmer's mother, credit couldn't be helped. You got the week's groceries on tick and paid for them when you could on pay day.

'It were Wednesday, pay day in t' mill, and she paid for last week's when she took this week's groceries. She'd say, 'Right, Mr Shaw, what do I owe you for last week?' And he'd get the book out and he'd say, 'Well, it's eighteen and six.' Right, and she'd pay him. And what she bought this week was on next week's book. And if she wanted anything else before next pay day, I used to go down to the shop for her and say, 'Put it on t' book.' Everyone did that. But you'd to be well-known and a good customer.'

Ron Carter had £60 redundancy money when the mill closed. But he had the works' anvil and set up as a blacksmith. He had to improve his own house first, so he made a staircase out of bits of metal tubing from the scrap yard, having taught himself to weld. 'And a builder came and said, 'I like this. Who's made it?' I said, 'Me'. He said, 'I want these in my houses – he was building 500 in Read, which was all downhill. So I said, 'I'll make them for you for £15 each.' And I did. And I used to deliver them on my bike. Can you imagine? I used to lean over, and Sheila, my wife, used to launch me down the hill. And when I got to 120 I could afford to buy a little mini-van.'

Ron's resourcefulness didn't stop at transporting staircases on a bike. He then decided he'd build his own house.

'Well, I thought. How do you build a house? I hadn't a clue about building. But I bought Fleetwood Pier that had burnt down. That's this floor we're on now. It had been under the sea for 103 years, that wood. But it's lovely wood. We did little deals like that. I bought second-hand bricks from Accrington Bricks. Anyway, I built it all. And then we flitted with a wheelbarrow. I remember the piano, we were all pushing it up this lane and one of the lads is playing it, "Home, Sweet Home".'

'You see, I'd spent £3,000 on materials, and that's what I'd sold the old house for. I didn't want a mortgage. I wanted to learn how to become a blacksmith properly. I wanted the odd day off looking at classical ironwork. I didn't want to be hand-to-mouth paying off a mortgage.'

These are heart-warming stories of Lancashire independence. True iron, wrought from a poor childhood where you learnt to value things, and tempered in the mill where you picked up prudence and resourcefulness. Where are these virtues now in this age of seductively easy credit and live-now-and-pay-later?

I've heard many stories of poverty amongst the smug affluence of today. Behind all the gloss of modern advertising and relentless consumerism, it's still around. Not the grinding poverty of those prematurely-aged figures in Waterside, returning hungry to their damp, dark hovels. But poverty hard to endure in an age when people are led to expect so much, and we're no longer all in the same boat but are confronted daily by images of wealth and excess.

I met Diane, who has been so skint she couldn't afford food. 'The day my daughter was born my partner lost his job because he wanted to be with me but his boss wanted him to work. We didn't have any money for five weeks and we had to beg food from our relatives. We had absolutely nothing. Christmas dinner consisted of soggy cream crackers. It was awful. I wanted to be dead.'

Cath described the plight of so many single mums today, caught between the devil of not being able to work for looking after their children and the deep blue sea of the bureaucratic and suspicious welfare services.

'I'm in a situation where I had to flee from this violent partner with nothing. I had to set up home with nothing. I needed a cooker, a fridge, beds, clothes, all sorts of things. Eventually, the DHSS agreed to loan me £1000. So now I'm permanently in debt to them. My outgoings are about £115 and my total income is £94 a week. So I can't afford to live each week. I can't go to work because I need five weeks' wage slips before I can get my child into child care. So what do I do for five weeks? Take the child to work with me?'

Bernadette is in a similar Catch 22. 'Last year I went out to work because I couldn't manage off benefits. But I wasn't any better off, so I stopped work. So I went to the DHSS, but because I didn't fill their forms in properly and they said I hadn't given them enough information, I had to live off £25, with two children and rent to pay.'

The temptation to take out credit in situations like this is often over-whelming. Melanie complains that the credit companies deliberately target the vulnerable:

'They send you forms and say, "Just fill it in". My sister has two kids and she's not working and she's got behind with her bills, so she's filled it in and now she's got a credit card which allows her to get over £500. And it gets people more into debt. Because they'll pay off their bills and then think they've still got money so they go out and get their kids new clothes and things, and it's more debt.'

But many of the second and third generation children of canny cotton weavers have inherited a suspicion of credit. As Diane Rogers told me. 'If you weren't sensible and level-headed, you could just go out tomorrow and get credit up to your eye-balls. You could get everything new. It's so easy. But there's no pleasure in it. It's easy come, easy go. And I can't stand loads of debt. That would make me ill.'

But as the century ends on a level of material affluence our forefathers could never have dreamt of when it began, I find it more encouraging to listen to stories from those who have turned their backs on material comforts and rediscovered some of the simpler pleasures of life. Cath Howley went to live in rural France with her children in the early 1990s.

'It was a beautiful place to live. I had everything I needed. I didn't have any money but we'd plenty of food in the freezers. We had hens and cows and we used to go fishing. We did lots of playing at being self-sufficient. We got up when the sun came up and went to bed when the sun went down. It was blissful. I used to walk around and dream. It was wonderful, just watching the trees come into flower with the different seasons and watching the birds. You can't believe how wonderful it was. And then going in and scrubbing the floor and making the house nice, and baking and gardening, catching wayward animals that had escaped, talking to the locals and swapping a dozen eggs for a round of brie, going and having an aperitif at 11 o'clock with the mayor in the village and strolling back. It was wonderful.'

A glimpse of how it was? A simple peasant life before we sold our labour in the mills and became forever enmeshed in the cash economy of getting and spending?

Arthur Garnett thinks he had his own Utopia when his children were young after the war:

'You looked after your family and paid all your bills and sometimes you had nowt, but you didn't go anywhere. We'd play cards on Sunday if it were raining and if it was fine you were up in the fields. And you worked for your family. You didn't work to swank that you'd got this and that. you cut your coat according to your pocket, and if you do that you'll live.'

Chapter Twelve

Playtime

'WE ONLY HAD half a childhood,' says Emma Edge, who has lived in every year of the twentieth century plus a couple from the last for good measure. We've heard how half-time working in the mill and domestic responsibilities soon brought childhood to an abrupt and premature end. It was an early apprenticeship that prepared them for a hard adult life. I'm always reminded when I listen to the stories of how hard people worked, of a phrase that so often appears on gravestones from those years: "At rest". It's a sad epitaph to a life that the only decent break you could look forward to was when you were in your coffin.

But if life was hard, when playtime came it brought an extra joy. And pleasures were simple. Basic acts of human fellowship stand out and are remembered. At 101, Emma Edge still remembers Tuesday night at the Bacup farmhouse when her brothers' pals all turned up for a sing-song. 'They could hear us in t' road,' Emma avows. And I've been to see where she lived and can vouch for it being half-a-mile from the road. Her mother played the harmonium and got a good ribbing from the youngsters. 'We used to say, my mother's playing t' Dead march, whenever she started, it were that slow.' It seems that youngsters have always found the musical tastes of their elders too conservative.

Organised entertainment was the strict preserve of the churches and chapels. Whitsun processions were a highlight of the somewhat limited social calendar. They made such an impression on the young Florrie Birtwell that today, at 95, she can still remember the exact route they took through Whalley. They'd meet up with other processions from all the other outlying villages, each with their own banner. A morning's walk was followed by dinner at the school then more processing through the abbey to the cricket field. 'And we were there playing games and running and the older ones dancing. And we had tea and we all joined together and there was dancing till dusk.'

Such Arcadian delights were taking place up and down the villages and towns of Lancashire at Whitsuntide. Colin Cooke remembers the procession in Sabden:

'Oh aye, they all dressed up, your best clothes on. And the banner, beautifully embroidered with the name of your church on, with tapes at either side, two at the front and two at the back, that people held. And if you went round a corner and the wind caught it, you'd to hang on.'

On the Church of England walking day – as opposed to the Methodist walking day – in Sabden, they were accompanied by a brass band. Colin recalls with a chortle that Sabden band 'was the only band that could play up-hill against the wind. They got some ale down before they started playing!'

Donald Barker was a bandsman. He remembers occasions when each church in the procession would have its own band. Once, when he played with the Tottington band, there were five others, all playing different tunes:

'It sounded terrible. 'T drummer was banging his drum as hard as he could, and they used to say, "Fill thi lungs and give it some stick, there's another band coming. We'll drown yon lot!"'

With the mills working a five-and-a-half day week until after the war, Sunday was the only full day for recreation. But for many, like Muriel Blenkinsop, the day was dominated by church and Sunday school attendance.

'You'd a busy time. We went to Sunday school in the morning followed by church. And in the afternoon you'd go to Sunday school again. A lot went. It was a big room with classes all the way round. They used to read a book to you or something like that. Then we went to church again at night. We'd more fun on a Sunday than most days of the week.'

But it wasn't fun for Doris Warburton who was born in 1902. 'It was like working. We got up and went to Sunday school at quarter-past-nine and we stayed for church which was half-past ten. We got home for lunch and were back in Sunday school at half-past one. That lasted until three o'clock. If you were a teacher there was a meeting that lasted till four. If you were a member of the choir, like I was, you went back at six o'clock and you were there till half-past seven. And that was your Sunday and you knew no other.'

But for Muriel Blenkinsop, the activities centred round her church were a delight.

'It used to be lovely at bazaar time. All these lovely stalls full of crafts and things that people used to make. And the Mothers' Union always made meat and potato pie suppers. And they'd come rolling in with great big washing-up bowls full of meat and potato pie with a suet crust on. And then there was a Sunday school party and a concert at night. And the hall was packed. It was all go.'

It wasn't just the churches that provided recreational fun. Florrie Birtwell remembers dos at the Co-op in Whalley.

'The Co-op used to make a lovely concert. There were six tables and six sittings, and we all used to have our tea and there'd be a concert afterwards. Or you could go to the Assembly Rooms where there was another concert. Then, if you got tired of that, you could come back to the Co-op for dancing.'

And there was something called a 'Scrap-eating Do', which seemed to involve polishing off the left-overs from another party, which I think we should do our best to revive, if only for its splendid name.

Sometimes the Sunday school would organise rambles. Emma Edge remembers one that took them from Bacup to Hardcastle Crags. They had a Good Friday breakfast up at the chapel – 'a knife-and-fork do with boiled

Whit walk: Boaters, Bonnets and Banners.

Whit walk. One of the highlights of the limited social calendar.

ham and tongue' – and then set off. 'We walked that much, the day after I couldn't get my shoes on, my feet were that swollen. But we enjoyed it.'

There's a naivety about these pleasures which could provoke some scorn from today's sybarites reared off the sophisticated leisure pursuits of our modern entertainment industry. But the very fact that they are recalled with such obvious delight after so many years – 90 in Emma's case – testifies to the joy they gave. How long, I wonder, will the offerings of Mr Murdoch's many Sky TV channels stay in the memory?

For all the blight cast by the cotton mills over our Lancashire valleys, such easy access to the countryside made us as much rural as urban creatures. Hettie Cunliffe and her young friends used to set off from Nelson and make a bee line for Pendle Hill. 'We always went what we call "hedge and dyke": we never walked on the roads but climbed over the hedges and across the fields. So we were at Pendle in half the time.'

I imagine outraged farmers brandishing hayforks, but Hettie is quick to assure me, 'We never did any harm. I was always brought up to reverence the countryside because all my family were farmers.'

So many farming folk had come into the towns in the last century to work in the mills, that these excursions into the countryside could be seen as a chance to refresh old roots; a return from the arid industrial townscape to drink at the crystal spring where they were born.

Country lore had not been forgotten in Florrie Birtwell's day, and people knew the names of trees and flowers:

'We used to walk every weekend, the whole family. We'd go from Wiswell to Pendleton and we'd talk and pick flowers to make buttonholes. There used to be wild strawberries in the dykes and primroses galore. The hedges used to be full.'

Sunday afternoon was the most popular time for walks. Arthur English, released from his weekday duties as dinner monitor in Maud Street in Barrowford, would set off for the Watermeetings or Roughlee:

'We only went to Pendle Hill on Good Friday. At Roughlee Lake they sold jugs of tea for sixpence and we'd take all our own food. When we went to the Watermeetings, there were hundreds and hundreds of families sat on the banking with all the little 'uns like us paddling and fishing in the river. I've seen thousands from the bridge at Roughlee on a Good Friday. You couldn't see the road for people. My granddad had an ice-cream business and on Good Friday we always took a cart with two tubs – normally we only had one tub in a cart – and we always went to the bottom of Pendle Hill. It was a long, long way in a horse and cart. But when we were going through Roughlee it was jam-packed full.'

In the valley milltowns the countryside is never very far away.

I know every area of Lancashire had its favourite country destination on a Good Friday and I'm sure many people will be able to provide their own details, but they will all have one thing in common: the vast numbers of townsfolk who undertook these excursions.

Just what it meant to people with such precious little leisure time to be free to roam the Pennine countryside is most famously illustrated in the passions aroused by the great Kinder Scout mass-trespass of the 1930s. Again, it's one of those important and written-about events that in recording a series like this you stumble across unexpectedly, not viewed from the perspective of one of the major protagonists but from a surprise witness, in this case, the young Ron Carter.

'I would only be about 14 in 1932 when they had this mass-trespass. All the hikers went to Hayfield to gather to go to Kinder Scout. I was told, "You can come but you haven't to go over the top because it might be dangerous." We walked up towards Kinder Scout and I had to stay behind near the reservoir while they went on. But I crept up behind them and saw what they were up to. And I remember a man speaking. He stood on a rock and addressed the whole lot about not being able to have access to all these wonderful moors, which they didn't want to damage but wanted the pleasure of walking over. And I remember my brothers telling me afterwards, that man was tried for inciting mutiny and he was put in gaol. And he was the most peaceful man that ever lived. A lovely guy. And on the jury I believe there were six colonels, four game-keepers and two men with stately homes!'

Margaret House, who was brought up in Charnock Richard remembers village entertainment in the late 1930s:

'We would have dances in the schoolroom and a band would come along and we'd all do the Palais Glide or the Military Two-step. And then there was a whist drive. I remember playing whist very well and winning quite a lot of prizes. You know, sacks of potatoes.'

Emma Edge's mother thought dancing was wicked and wouldn't let her go. But Emma was allowed out on a Saturday night to the pictures. She was given threepence: a penny to go in, a penny for a vanilla at the interval and ha'peth of chips on the way home. 'We thought it were wonderful!'

Alice Lambert and her friend Mary Warren remember queuing up at the Savoy pictures in Colne. Seats were tuppence and they both remember Harriet Greenwood playing the piano to accompany the silent films:

'When it was cowboys and Indians, she was going mad on the piano. But if it were a pathetic little love story it was all slow and sentimental.'

Saturday afternoon matinees were always a boisterous affair for Arthur

Garnett and his chums. 'We'd stand outside queuing up for the penny seats which were right at the front. And as soon as the lights went down, we crept back into the better seats. And then Old Joe would come with his flashlight and move us back. But as soon as his back was turned we were off again.

'You couldn't go in t' circle if you'd clogs on,' recalls Colin Cooke. 'There was a bloke with a peaked cap and he had a big stick. He used to give you a tap and knock you into line. Sometimes someone would roll a bottle down the aisle and he'd put the lights on and clear the place. If there was anyone marlicking he'd get right mad and clear the row out. If a goody was chasing a baddy we'd be standing up and cheering like at a football match. And we used to talk about it all the way home as we walked, three miles from Padiham.'

Sport drew huge audiences. When Nelson played Bacup in 1931 there were 14,000 spectators down Seedhill cricket ground. 'There were as many

Emma Edge's mum, centre back, and a group of Bacup farmers' wives who used to hold 'surprise tea parties' to raise money for food parcels to the troops during the Great War.

A Turf Moor league football crowd, around 1914.

watching them practise as you get at league games today,' says Ken Hartley. They'd to put special nets up to keep the crowds back from the net practices. The star attraction in the 1930s was the Nelson professional Learie Constantine. His wonderful performances lifted people. 'It took them away from the drudgery of cotton weaving and the insecurity that was in the area at that time.'

A decade later it was Stanley Matthews who was drawing the crowds to league football matches. Arthur English recalls that Burnley generally played Blackpool on Boxing Day. 'We got to Burnley and the road up to the football field: you couldn't see it for people. And when we got there, they'd locked the gates and we couldn't get in.'

Inside the ground, people stood on the ash which had come out of the mill boilers:

'It was nothing but ash on two sides from the pitch right up to the top, and that's how they could get 40,000 on. It were wonderful. And they used to pass little lads like me over their heads and put us over the wall at the front to see. And if anybody fainted or was taken ill, everybody round about pulled out their handkerchieves and waved to the St John's Ambulance men who would come running round with a stretcher. Of course, they were hankies then, not paper tissues.'

'There was no fighting at all. On Boxing Day later on in the 50s, Newcastle generally came and they used to bring a load with them. And we all used to go on the Longside, and there we all were, all stood together, Newcastle and Burnley, singing Blaydon Races. It was wonderful. And I've never been since they sold Jimmy McIlroy.'

Wakes Week holidays are a major slice of Lancashire folk lore today. It's hard to imagine such a mass exodus as there was to Blackpool and Morecambe when the mills shut down for a week in the summer. But you can forget Morecambe, there was only one place as far as Arthur English and scores of thousands of other families were concerned:

'You could say that Nelson and Barrowford nearly all moved to Blackpool, anybody who could afford. Everybody was there with their suitcases waiting for the bus to the station. "Where are you going?" "Blackpool. Blackpool. Blackpool." And then when we got off the bus there were all these lads with trucks and home-made trolleys waiting to carry your bag to the station for tuppence. And there were so many people, they'd only let you onto the platform in certain numbers because it was full up. But in another ten minutes there was another train, and there was no question about where it was going.'

'You knew everybody on the train going to Blackpool,' recalls Eileen Cook from Colne. 'And they'd be saying, "Are you going to Mrs So-and-so's? We're going to Mrs Hardcastle's." You took your own food and paid for the "cruet", they used to say, because they charged you so much for doing your cooking. And your mother would go out at the morning and shop. And this was always a mystery to me: she might get some stuff for you, but there'd be about five other families staying at your boarding house, and you had your own little cupboard in the dining room. And your mother would go in and say, "Well, this is our steak and some potatoes and peas", and someone else would take sausage, and someone else would happen take chops. Well, how did she cook for all these people and not get 'em mixed up? It allus used to amaze me did that.'

'And when you went out on t' prom, you'd say, "Hello! Ee, Hello!" You might as well have just stopped in Colne because everybody knew everybody. All one town had gone that one holiday week.'

'They all wanted to see one another when they got there,' says Arthur English. 'The general routine was: Central Pier in the morning because there was dancing and all the amusements that were going on. Afternoon on the sands. There'd be many a football match between different mills in Nelson or Barrowford on Blackpool sands. But it would be 22 a side, not 11. And on the last night, Friday, we'd go to the Pleasure Beach and spend up.'

Wakes week crowd at Padiham Station.

It's easy to be blasé about holidays such as this these days when a day-trip to Blackpool is part of everyone's experience from early childhood. But to hear Eddie Hothersall describing his first sight of the sea and rushing off home to hold a rapt audience in the school playground as he recounts his adventure, is to share an innocent sense of wonder lost to a more sophisticated age.

'I'd never seen the sea before. I mean, it looked so big. I'd only be 11 or 12 and it looked huge. As far as you could see, water. I thought, just imagine living here and coming out every day and seeing all this water and all this sand. It was great. And it lasted for weeks, the memories. You were telling everybody at school and they were all clustered round. Happy days!'

Alice Whittle's Grandfather Taylor had a problem when he went to Morecambe. He got violent headaches and was sick. When he visited the doctor, he was solemnly told, 'It's the air. It's too bracing.' On one occasion Alice was out with him and her father in a boat in the bay fishing for fluke when a squall blew up. Granddad was sick and his false teeth disappeared

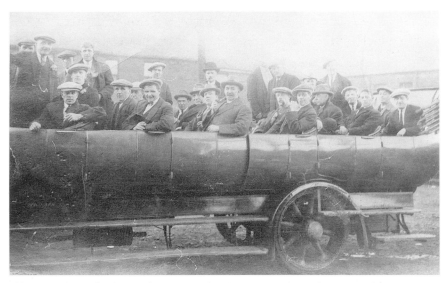

Above: Trip to Blackpool from Grimshaw's Brewery, Burnley, around 1930. Not much room for the bottles in the back.

Below: School trip 1923. Off for their first glimpse of the sea?

into the sea. For 70 years the image has endured with Alice of both men vainly fishing around in Morecambe Bay trying to retrieve granddad's teeth.

If you didn't go to Blackpool or Morecambe you were considered posh and got talked about in the Co-op. 'If anyone went to Torquay or Bournemouth,' remembers Doris Warburton, who lived in a village in the Rossendale Valley, 'they were discussed in the Co-op for a fortnight. They'd got above themselves.'

What they made of Pete Bradshaw in Padiham when in the early 1960s he announced that he and his mates were going on a package holiday to Spain is lost to posterity. This must have been one of the first package holidays of its kind in the area. It cost £19 for a fortnight and involved a coach trip from Central Motors in Padiham and camping.

'Nobody in Padiham had been to Spain then. We drove down to Dover, crossed the Channel and went to Paris. And all our tents were in the boot. We had to put these tents up and nobody had done it before. If you could have filmed us, you'd have got three series of "Game for a Laugh". And this happened three nights running until we got to Spain. But when we got to Lorette, the tents were already up. I loved it. I mean, going from Padiham with its smoky chimneys and freezing cold and constant rain. It opened my eyes. And things were so cheap. A St Miguel was 8 pesetas and we were getting 160 pesetas to the pound. We thought it was marvellous. And there were bars that stayed open till one or two in the morning. Everything in Padiham shut at half-past ten!'

But the world had started to come to North East Lancashire by the late 1950s – the world of entertainment. Pat Berry remembers all the top bands coming to the Imperial Ballroom in Nelson. 'Geraldo, Ted Heath, Johnny Dankworth, I've seen them all down t' Imp. They used to have a different ball every Friday. There'd be the Policeman's Ball, the Fireman's Ball, the Ambulance Ball, and everybody used to go. It was between eight and one, and the place was heaving. Heaving. I'll bet half of Nelson and Colne in those days met their wives or husbands down t' Imp. And there used to be a boppers' corner where we used to bop our socks off. I've had some rare times at the Imp.'

'And then along came Elvis,' recalls Margaret McLean, as if signalling the arrival of an earthquake. 'Rock and roll changed the whole face of music. Our parents couldn't cope. Let's face it. There was no such thing as a teenager until the late 50s. And we'd turn the music up at full on the radio and be bopping, and it drove our parents to distraction. I'll never forget when Jailhouse Rock came to the Empire in Burnley. They rove the pictures to bits. And my dad was there! He was off work ill and we persuaded him to go and see it. And he went absolutely mad about it. He was furious. We loved it! When we went dancing we had about four underskirts on, and we used to wash them in a bowl of sugar to make them so stiff so they stuck out. When you sat down it nearly covered your face.'

'Dress was wonderful,' says Cath Howley, slipping into something different and the swinging sixties. 'We used to wear white plastic boots and mini skirts and huge dangling earrings. And hair! I went from having plaits at 14 to cutting the lot off, the Greek urchin look. It meant coming home from school every night and chopping a bit more off with the nail scissors. Lots of black mascara and eye shadow and white lipstick. It was Twiggy and wonderful and it caused such a stir. Parents hated it. I used to run down the drive, hide behind the garden wall, put the make-up on and reverse the procedure when I came back. It was really hard getting it all off again.'

Crowded pubs, all-night parties, blaring discos – the 70s and 80s merge into a whirl of wild hedonism. But as youth grew wilder, the older end retreated more and more into their own firesides. Television arrived, as the Rossendale-born Bishop of Sheffield observed, and people participated less and less in life. No more Whit walks, field days or Scrap-eating Dos.

'I don't call that a benefit, I call it a monster,' says 77 year-old Mary Cockle of television. 'It's spoilt family life. It can make people lonely, you know. And they're fastened up to these soaps like Coronation Street and Neighbours and such like. And the only thing that keeps things like that going is falling out. Who wants that? I don't. I don't watch 'em. I'd be bothered what I was missing on t' radio.'

I say Amen to that.

≈ *Chapter Thirteen* ≈

Going Places

$\mathcal{A}$s YOU LISTEN to old people talking about their lives, sometimes a picture takes shape in your mind which will stay there forever. Colin Wiseman drew one such indelible picture. Colin is 90 and was reared in the village of Twiston in the northern shadow of Pendle Hill. He remembers the buttercarts that used to bring their dairy produce into the milltown of Nelson, over the bare moors past the steep end of Pendle, over Black Moss, and down from Blacko Bar into the town. The road is dusty and unmade up, just limestone held together by rainwater. As the horse and cart ambles along, people pass on foot and exchange a greeting. A traveller on horseback waves. It could be a scene out of one of the novels of Thomas Hardy, rural England as it has been for hundreds of years.

And then the cart comes down into Barrowford where the tramlines begin. The horse grows nervous. There's the grinding of metal against metal as a tram goes past. Clogs clatter on the cobbles as people hurry past. There's the muffled roar of the looms from the mills by the riverside, the silver glint of a steam piston jabbing ceaselessly, all the noise and clatter and self-importance of a sophisticated and successful mechanical age. We have entered the twentieth century.

The reason why this picture will remain unforgettable to me is because it's a journey between two ages. Between a rural past of slow carts and horses and walking distances that has changed little since the invention of the wheel, and today's world of startling speeds and mechanical transport-ation. And I can't really get it into my head that both worlds can exist side by side within the experience of one lifetime; that we can still listen to people like Colin who are a living, breathing link with distant history.

'From Twiston there were two buttercarts went to Nelson and they used to take the butter and the eggs. And they'd take wild mushrooms when there were any to be got and maybe a few rabbits. And they'd also carried things like your boots and your clogs to be soled and bring them back the same day. And you'd meet people walking. There were more

A coalman stops to encourage a stubborn donkey.

people in the country then knocking about than there are today. And there were quite a few people on horseback. Horse transport was everything in those days. But, of course, the horses that pulled the buttercarts were very frightened of the trams. They didn't see them, only when they went over there. And when you got to Barrowford, all the roads were setts, and it was very bad for them. It was very hard for them and used to hurt them above their hooves and eventually they had to take them off because they went lame.'

But when motorised transport did make an appearance in the neighbourhood, it didn't make much of an impression on Colin Wiseman:

'And then motorcars started coming along about 1920. They were all short of power and Twiston was all steep hills and they got stuck. They'd come from the provender firms and the drivers had to come up to the farms and say, 'Will you bring your horse and cart and take your proven

An incredible load for 2 horse-power: logs going to make timber for canal barges around the turn of the century.

off my motor.' And I used to think they were a dead loss these motors. I thought, they'll never be any use. We're better off with these Clydesdales and shire horses that we had.'

Ben Barnes' grandfather had as many as 60 horses for his transport business in Rawtenstall. But having all those horses didn't make hauling finished cotton cloth to Manchester any quicker.

'They used to have to set off about midnight on a Sunday night to get to Manchester for 8 o'clock next morning. They might have 5 or 6 tons in two carts, and when they came to a steep hill like the one going up to Edenfield, they would take one cart to the top of the hill and return for the other. And they had to have a chain horse to help the other two out on the hills. So sometimes, if they were going during the week, they'd break their journey at the Mason's Arms in Whitefield and stable the horses and set off to Manchester next morning. If they were travelling on a cold night they'd have glasses of rum left out for them on the kitchen window bottom. My dad would go in, lift the window and put tuppence down for

Slow progress up the hill into Colne.

it. The landlord had gone to bed. But everyone was honest and always paid up.'

But even proceeding at the pace of a carthorse didn't mean you escaped the attentions of the law. Ben Barnes's sister, Margaret Creamer, remembers their father telling her: 'Coming down Bacup Road at Clough Fold there was always a policeman standing in a doorway waiting to see if they could catch the drivers asleep and summons them.' 'And it wasn't just a question of being asleep,' says Ben:

'They used to leave a space on the corner of the cart to sit on, and if it was raining they could pull the sheet over their heads and still see where the horses were going. But if a policemen came along and he was under the sheet, he was classed as being asleep and fined 5 shillings for not being in charge of the horse.'

Ben remembers being taken up into the fields as a five-year-old to where the horses were rested over the week end:

Loading woven cloth on to a horse-drawn cart.

'They used to run wild in these fields once they'd let them go. And when they brought them down again on Sunday afternoon to brush them down and get them ready for wherever they were going that night, my father used to put me on top of one to ride down. Some of them were rough horses to handle but they wouldn't go through the stable door and slough me off their backs. They'd wait outside until someone took me off. And they all had names, like Captain and Queenie. There were loads of names. You'd get gypsies coming wanting to buy them or sell you one. Many a time my father would buy one and fatten it up by feeding it well. It was nothing in those days to give a horse a bucket of beer if it wasn't feeling well. Baxter's Brewery was on the corner and we used to get a lot of barrels of beer that were past their sell-by date.'

But it wasn't drunkenness but steam wagons that finished off the horses. Ben's father bought several of the machines in 1920 but he still used horses for local deliveries and bringing coal out of the railway sidings. And some of the older drivers didn't want anything to do with the new transport, so it was 1929 or 30 before the horses trooped out. And by this time the Barneses were buying petrol wagons.

Arthur Garnett sounds to have had as much trouble going uphill with his petrol wagon as the Barneses did with their horses:

'You didn't drive 'em above 20 miles per hour. I always remember my dad going to Haworth cemetery with a load of bricks, and you'd get going over the tops and when you got half-way up, you had to stop because the wagon would start to boil. You used to pull up at the side of the road and get out onto the grass and have a smoke while it cooled off. You were lucky to do three trips a day from the Borough Brick Company in Nelson to Haworth 12 miles away.'

Further afield, the journey to Scotland held the daunting prospect of climbing Shap. But there was an element of exhibitionism about Ben Barnes' approach:

'You'd be in bottom gear. Many a time, the bloke I had with me, Jim Pilling, who'd been gassed in the 14–18 War, used to think nothing of getting out and walking at the side of the lorry while you got to the top of Shap. I've seen me put a brick on the accelerator and stand up on t' doorway and have a wee while the motor was still climbing Shap.'

Those trams which so frightened the buttercart horses were a welcome means of free transport to George Howarth. 'I'd no money so I'd get to Nelson on the back of a tram. I waited for it to stop at Elm Street and there was a fender at the back and I used to sit on there holding t' big lamp. Every time it stopped I got off and jumped on again just before it set off. I got to Nelson that way.'

The last of the trams, 1934.

Trams meet buses meet solitary horse and cart, Burnley, around 1932.

You can still see some of the high-spirited youngster in Eddie Hothersall today, even though he's 77. Young Eddie loved trams because on some of them the polished wooden seats ran longways down one side and when the tram pulled up sharp he enjoyed a good slide. When the buses started to replace them, it was a real novelty. If Eddie was waiting for a tram and a bus arrived, there was high excitement. 'Oh, it's a bus! A bus!' he'd yell, even though they didn't clang and clatter like a tram, though they must have still been bone-shakers, running on the cobbled streets with solid tyres fitted to the back wheels – only the front ones were pneumatic.

Margaret Creamer remembers her father having three wagons with solid tyres that were brought into the farm barn on a Friday and the flat bodies used for carrying cloth were replaced by coach bodies ready to take people out on pleasure trips at the weekend:

'There was a door to every row and one of my jobs as a girl was to clean all the brass handles. They had a hood which covered the seats when it rained, but they were open at the sides so the passengers had to take umbrellas. The wagons had names. There was Our Mag, Lady Phyllis and Lady Mary, all named after members of the family.'

Ben Barnes recalls coach trips to Blackpool:

'They used to think nothing of setting off at about 7 o'clock in the morning. My father would be there and folk would come down and he'd say, "Are you going to Blackpool?" And they'd say, "No, it's raining." And my dad would say, "Well, I'll tell you what do. Give us ten bob for t' lot of you and if it's not fine by the time we get to Kirkham, I'll give you your money back." And invariably by the time they got to Kirkham it would be fine and he'd keep his ten bob note. It took about three hours to go to Blackpool. Then they got going to Morecambe and Southport and Scarborough came into it and Llandudno, but that was an overnight job. Because invariably the magneto would go and there were certain parts he had to stop and grease.'

Betty Moore was regularly sent from her home in Liverpool to stay with relatives in London and travelled on her own by coach. She was only a child:

'We were always having minor accidents or getting lost in fog and we once had a three-coach crash. I never expected to arrive in London in one piece but we did. The coach once caught fire on the way back from London. I can remember wearing a beaver lamb coat which had been cut down and leather gloves with a beaver lamb backing. And the next thing, flames started coming out of the engine and we had to get out quickly and it was raining like mad. I sat on a boulder in the rain while we waited for another coach to come. And when I got home I sobbed my heart out. Everybody thought it was because of the accident, but no, it was because I'd lost one of my gloves.'

Driving tests were not very stringent when Ben Barnes took his in 1939.

'I had to go to Burnley, and I drove down on my own, I didn't know I'd to take anyone with me. And the examiner said, "Has anyone come with you?" I said, "No, I've come on my own." "Well, you're supposed to have someone with you that can drive. We'll say that So-and-so came with you." Then he said, "Right, do you know where the railway station is? Well, take me there." And then when he'd got out he said "You've passed." I'd actually taken him to the station so that he could go home.'

The railway tunnels are all bricked up today on the line that used to run down from Bacup to Waterfoot through what is called The Glen and used to be known as the Thrutch. It's hard to imagine the chaotic scenes at Waterfoot station at Wakes Week as the trains arrived to take everyone to Blackpool.

'We'd put our suitcases on a farmer's cart that was taking milk down to the station,' says Donald Barker. 'They'd be lined up all down the

Lost options. The railway line from Colne to Skipton passes over a busy Leeds & Liverpool Canal at Foulridge Wharf.

platform and as son as the train came through the tunnel there'd be such a rush forward. There'd be ten or twelve in a compartment with their luggage as well, sat on one another's knees, some of the smaller kids laid on the luggage racks above. No corridors. I've seen them weeing through open windows, and when we came to a station there'd be a mass exodus.'

Fred Smith was a fireman on the railways and recalls there being as many as 300 trains running into Blackpool Central on a summer weekend. He used to run Saturday night Dance Specials to the resort. They had to make do with an old engine built in the 1880s and 10 antiquated suburban coaches without toilets.

'Coming home it was 12 midnight out of Blackpool. And nine times out of ten you got stopped outside Preston Junction to allow the main-line London–Glasgow express through. And as soon as you stopped, you could hear the carriage doors being opened and the lights from the carriages shining on the ground. And little did they realise how far it is from the carriage floor to the ground. And they were jumping out, fellows and ladies, and dashing off into the fields to pee. But they couldn't get back, it was that high up. And we must have left dozens every Saturday night around Preston. And I've often wondered to myself, "How did they get back to Burnley, Nelson and Colne, because we were the last train? And how did they get across a busy junction without being knocked down or getting their feet trapped in the points?" I used to ask the driver, "What happens to them?" And he said, "I couldn't care less." And we went.'

John Holt from Colne was another fireman but he drove the big expresses on the main line up to Scotland. When it came to the express trains, you can forget horses and carts and rattling trams. This was speed in the way we understand it today.

'When you're on a train with maybe 16 or 17 coaches on and a thousand people inside it and you got that running along in excess of 100 mph, it was a thrill indeed. I mean, these hills you had to work hard to get up, like Beattock and Shap, you also came down them. You'd be a couple of minutes late at the top of Shap but you'd be on time going through Oxenholme. You daren't look into the fire because it was incandescent. It would sent you blind. We didn't have cushion tyres on, you'd to dance to shovel coal and keep your balance. You were being thrown about and you'd to hang on to something if you were stood up. The noise was out of this world. Everything had a rhythm. It was like Dante's Inferno to music. It was the biggest realisation of speed it was possible to get. We used to work the fastest train in England, the newspaper train for Glasgow from Manchester at night. And near Tebay we used to pass the postal train going in the opposite direction. And it had a series of white lights down the side of it. And it used to go "Whap!" and you'd passed it in a flash. And going through Tebay at the foot of Shap, the faster you went through there, the less effort it took to get over Shap. And I used to love it.'

Ben Barnes graduated to better and more reliable coaches, but the customers didn't improve. One of his biggest headaches was trying to prise drinking parties out of the pub in order to get home to his wife and family at a civilised hour. They were an incorrigible lot. Once they'd thoroughly wet their whistles, you could have announced the end of the world and they'd have stayed for another.

'One of my first experiences with a drunken party was in a pub at the other side of Settle. Their plans were to be back at their club in Burnley by nine o'clock to have the last hour there. So I sat in the coach, and about nine o'clock I started the engine up and I went in and I said, "Are you ready?" "Nay," they said. They were darting away. you could see they'd no intention of moving. Anyway, I knocked the engine off, and about half-past ten there was a bobby came on a push-bike. Of course, then pubs were supposed to shut at ten. So I thought, when he goes in, they'll come out of there like chickens out of a hen cote. So I started the engine up again. Anyway, about half-past eleven I went in, and t' bobby has his coat off and he's darting away and they're plying him with drink – whisky, you name it. And it must have been half-past twelve or one o'clock when they came out of this pub. And I were that mad, I'd undone his handlebars on his bike and put them where the seat should have been and the seat where the handlebars were. And when I went in, everybody was too tipsy to do owt with this bobby and make him look presentable, so t' landlord and me put his uniform on back-to-front and buttoned it down t' back. We loaded him in the coach and hung his bike on the back, and I laid him out on one of the market stalls in Settle and away we came home.'

'Funnily enough, it was months before I went through Settle again, but when I did it was market day and we generally stopped at Ye Olde Naked Man for a cup of tea when we were going to Morecambe. And this bobby were on point duty. Well, he kept looking at the coach and looking at me, he must have had me waiting five minutes before he waved me onto the car park. I think he had a bit of an idea it was me, but he didn't say anything.'

Ben Barnes' tales would fill a book of their own. Stories of whole coach parties answering the call of nature at the roadside, women as well as men. But chivalry bids me draw a modest veil over such matters.

Today's holidays abroad, where jet travel is commonplace, make those early stories of slow and uncomfortable travel sound as though they belong to a different millennium. But quite a few people I've spoken to have grave misgivings about the speed of progress in travel.

Roy Ashworth, who loves to walk the highlands and islands of Scotland, hates the way the world has been constricted by air travel. Working with VSO, he has witnessed how tourism can spoil places. He deplores African safari holidays:

'They call it "Zoo Africa" now. There's a constant stream of Land Rovers with people with too much money in their pockets. I've slept out in the bush myself, but what they do isn't genuine.' He points out the artificiality of the people who fly out to the Philippines to be entertained by locals dancing in grass skirts whose day job is in a bank. And in Antigua, he has witnessed the effect of the 'haves' arriving amongst the 'have-nots', in the upsurge of violence and crime.

'It's making the world so much smaller. When you think of England, it used to be a huge country 200 years ago. It would take you a fortnight to get to Glasgow. Now it's just an overcrowded little midden.'

But the loudest criticism is reserved for the motor car, that liberator turned gaoler. People find themselves gridlocked more and more. What used to be a simple journey to work has now become a test of patience and endurance. Small villages have become choked with parked motorcars and double lines have spread like yellow fever.

Chris Johnson, the organic food specialist from Ramsbottom, blames this on our rejection of public transport. He met a frazzled-looking customer of his recently. '"I'll be glad when I get my car back," he said. "It's taken me an hour to get from Manchester on the bus." And I said, "But at this time it takes you an hour-and-a-half to get here in the car." "Ah, yes," he said. "But I'm in control of that." How stupid – sorry if he recognises himself – but how bloody stupid! We're clogging our roads up, polluting our lungs, wasting so much time driving around in silly little cars that have windows that go up and down when you press a button and feeling ever so grand when you sit up in a Range Rover looking down on somebody in a little Ford car. Stupid prats!'

I don't know how many Range Rovers sweep along the tarmacked roads today between Twiston and Nelson where the buttercart used to amble along, but Colin Wiseman's forecast that the motor car was a dead loss and would never be any use, turned out to be horribly wrong. To our cost.

~ *Chapter Fourteen* ~

Life and Death

$\mathcal{A}$T NINETY-FOUR, Lizzie Hartley sits in her front room in her terraced house in Colne weighing you up shrewdly. It isn't long before she has a cure for all your ailments. Her favourite nostrum is something called skull-cap and valerian, which has a distinct feel of crooked old ladies living alone in forest clearings, to me. Which isn't too wide of the mark, because Lizzie's dad was a herbalist, and 85 years ago he had his daughter making up his pills and patent medicines.

Lizzie Hartley, brim-full of vitality at 94.

'I used to sit on a buffet and he'd start off: liquorice, essence of peppermint, pennyroyal, essence of juniper – and other ingredients I am under oath not to divulge – and he'd mix it all together like he was baking. And then when he'd got it to a roll, he'd break a bit off and he'd say, "Now, you have to make these pills round. Think on!" And he made me do these pills perfectly round and he sold 'em at a shilling a box. And they came from far and wide to buy them!'

This is a time when the word pharmaceutical would have brought a look of blank incomprehension. Everyone had their own homespun cure for everything. Talk to people from this generation and the old remedies come tumbling out like dead moths from a wardrobe.

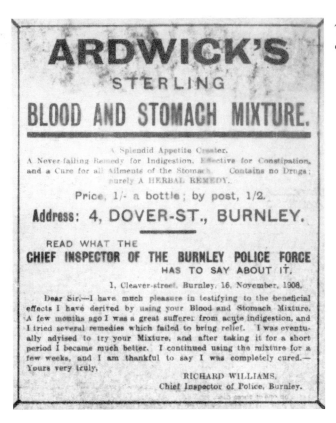

Top cop backs
quacks.

Ethel Howarth's grandfather was a kind of witch doctor too:

'He could do anything. If you had a cut on your finger that wouldn't stop bleeding, he would get a cobweb to put on it. For an old sore that wouldn't heal up he'd get some mould from an old shoe and it would soon get better.'

'If they had anything festering,' says Agnes Cross, who was brought up on a farm in the Fylde, 'they used to put on soft soap and sugar, or fat bacon, that was a good drawing thing.'

Children seem to have spent winter time embalmed in all sorts of weird and wonderful concoctions. 'If we'd a cough,' says Agnes, 'my mother used to put us a brown paper on our chests and it was covered in camphorated oil and grated nutmeg.' 'I used to have tonsillitis a lot,' says Ethel Howarth, 'and my mother used to boil some potatoes and put them in a sock and put them round my neck, and then you squeezed them and all the steam came out.' I bet she tasted grand with a couple of sausages and some gravy.

If you could survive all the home cures in those days you were destined for a long and healthy life. In Ben Barnes' family, the cure for boils sounds worse than the affliction:

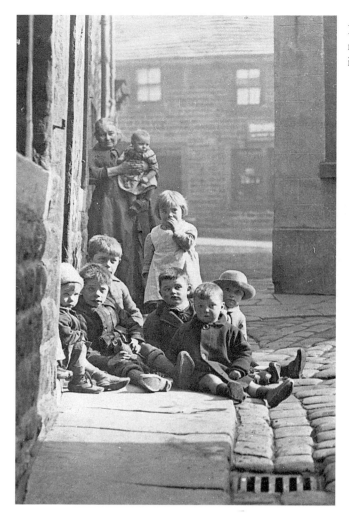

Poverty was a root cause of illness and disease.

'One of the finest things you could have for boils was a spoonful of soot from up the chimney. You used to mix it up in some milk and drink it and, by gum, after three or four of those your boils would start to go!'

Ethel Howarth concludes: 'Everybody knew some remedy if you had something wrong with you. You got better but it took longer and you didn't have any drugs. You see, you had to pay to go to the doctor, and those that could afford used to pay a shilling a week to the doctor's man who used to come round on a Friday night. That way, if you were ill you had some money to pay the doctor. But most people helped one another and you'd use stuff that you had in the house to get better. But, of course, folks died as well. In those days it was the survival of the fittest.'

But poverty was a root cause of illness and disease, and in those days people wore their poverty on their backs:

Damside, Colne, in all its dinginess.

'You could tell by everybody's clothes who was better off than others,' says Muriel Blenkinsop, brought up in Bolton in the 1920s. 'I can remember two boys in particular in our class at school and they did live in a very poor street. They weren't bad lads but I can remember them looking rough, with holes in their jerseys and shoes. And since I've grown up, I've thought they got picked on by the teachers. I can remember feeling sorry for them. And I can also remember this girl and she did smell a bit – it's a horrible smell when people smell. And she was very poor, and even now I can see lice walking up her neck as she bent over her desk.'

'One thing used to stick in my mind as a school lad,' recalls Donald Barker, 'was the children who used to come into school sopping wet with no decent shoes on. And all round Water school, there were thick six-inch pipes and their clothes were put all round there to dry, and t' stench were terrible.'

But the enduring image of poverty is the one we've heard already from Titus Thornber, of the Burnley slums he had to walk through, with excrement emptied into the streets and children playing in the gutters. Just the situation that gave rise to the scourge of diseases like diphtheria.

As a young policemen in Burnley, Lynn Millard recalls that it was the police force that was put in charge of the fever ambulance:

'They used to have a separate brown ambulance which was kept at the fire station and was only used for infectious diseases. Now if anybody got diphtheria or scarlet fever and they took them away in the ambulance, children were told not to watch and to stay away from the house. 'And don't play around grates,' we were told as children. 'Never play around grates.'

Barbara Hastie's seven-year-old sister succumbed to the dreadful disease.

'She was a very open-air child was Marion, never ailing anything. Short, fair-haired, a wonderful natured child. But she used to play in these out-houses, and I wonder if it was that. Anyway, she started on the Saturday and said she wasn't well and she had a sore throat. And she never complained. She went to bed early on the Saturday night and on the Sunday her neck was swollen right out here. Anyway, she gradually got worse and worse and my dad rang the doctor on Monday morning. Well, the doctor didn't come until the evening and when he did he brought a nurse with him. And they were whispering, and he said, "She must go to the hospital right away. It's diphtheria." And they started flapping around with red blankets and the ambulance came and took her away.'

'At the hospital my mum had to be all gowned and masked up and she sat with her. She was in a steam tent but she was unconscious and they'd done a tracheotomy on her because she couldn't breathe. It didn't look like her at all. She looked as though she was twenty, not seven. Anyway, my mother hadn't been sat there long before she turned blue and my mother called the nurse and she passed away.'

'Now, we weren't allowed to bring her home. They let the hearse draw up at the door but you weren't allowed to bring them in. And they came and fumigated the bedroom. They sealed all the windows and doors, and it was like a gas and it ruined all your things. After that, there were four children in the neighbourhood got it but two of them survived. And they turned away from us, did people, because they thought it was our fault. But we were just unfortunate, weren't we?'

Betty Moore was only seven when she went into hospital in 1928 for an operation. She's never forgotten the operating theatre:

'I was taken in on a trolly in my nightie – my parents had not been allowed to visit – and the first thing I saw was a glass cabinet with all sorts of instruments and God knows what. And when they laid me down on

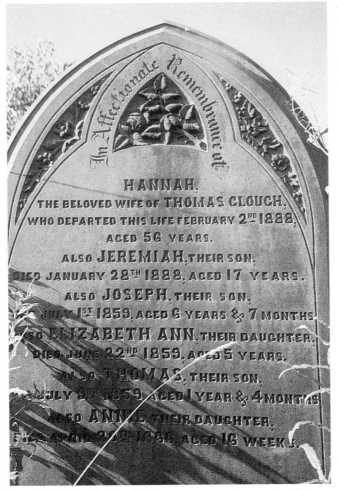

This gravestone at Haggate near Burnley is a shocking monument to child mortality in the old days.

the operating table there were all these knives and scissors and funny things lined up. It's always stayed with me because it was the worst episode of my life.'

For Judith Rowan, operated on as a child after contracting polio in the 1950s, 'it was a terrifying experience. You knew something awful was going to happen but you'd no idea what. Nobody sat down and talked to you. But the day of the operation, I can remember sitting there reading the Bible with all these figures around me, nurses rushing past, women in candlewick dressing gowns moaning away about this and that. It was really frightening for a child. And then they came and put you in all this regalia: the gown, the turban, the socks, and they put you on the trolley and took you down to the theatre. They put me on the operating table, all these lights overhead, these masked and gowned figures, and they put the

A butcher's shop to make today's environmental health inspectors blanch.

chloroform over my face. I remember the stink of it, the smell of the rubber, the lights swinging overhead. And I just fought like hell because I thought I was going to die. There's a roaring in your ears and you can feel yourself slipping away, and I thought I'd never see my parents again. It was awful.'

People had a more robust attitude to health in the old days than we have today. Perhaps the absence of the media with their daily dose of health scare stories made them less neurotic. George Rushton, farming after the war on the edge of Burnley, when practically every farm had its own milk round, remembers people being very philosophical about the risk from untreated milk:

'I think there was an acceptance of food-transmitted diseases that we wouldn't tolerate now. TB was fairly widespread in cattle and there was always a danger of picking it up from the milk or even the meat of infected animals. It was maybe that people didn't think too much about the risk, like people today who smoke.'

Hilda Parkinson, now 69, epitomises this outlook. 'I used to drink milk straight out of the cow. We'd no cooling system so I drank it straight out of the bucket. It was good. I was brought up that way and I've not done so bad off it, have I?'

Nevertheless, sanitary conditions in places where food was sold were

The canal in Burnley today. In the past canal suicides often took place close to the mills where the water was warmer.

enough to give a modern environmental health officer an apoplexy. Colin Cooke began butchering at the age of fourteen during the war:

'There weren't so many fridges. We used to have an ice box, like a coffin lined with metal which you put ice in. We'd get a 28lb block from Padiham and it came on top of the coal wagon – are you listening for hygiene? – and when he got to the butchers' shops, he threw it out on the setts at the front of the shop and I went out with a hammer, broke it up, put it in a bucket and threw it on top of the ice box. If it were hot, it would only last for a day. But in those days, folk bought something, took it home and ate it the same day. Not like today, putting it in the freezer and keeping it a week or two or eating half and putting half back in the fridge. That's why there's all these problems today. Now, the meat at a butchers was hung outside on t' wall. And I used to have a fly swatter. Ee, there were flies as big as Jack Russells. I used to go out banging 'em with this big fly swatter. But nobody ailed owt. I can't remember anyone having food poisoning.

Beelzebub was a regular customer at Tom Kennedy's fish stall on Blackburn Market:

'Oo, flies! By gum, there used to be some flies! You used to stand there with a newspaper wafting them off. I mean, I've seen, when you've missed a bit of fish in the corner when you've been cleaning down on Saturday night, come back Monday morning, and it would just be a moving ball of maggots!'

Tom doesn't remember people being ill either. 'Everybody's ill nowadays. They're all suffering from some allergy or another. They're not eating enough muck. They're not! They're looking after themselves too much. I don't remember killing anyone with rotten fish. And I'm sure their relations would have told me about it!'

He tells one good story about a very nonchalant stallholder:

'There was a chap on the next stall to me who was a right old timer. He never took his pipe out of his mouth, even when he was serving – smoking were good for you in those days, it cleared your pipes. And a woman came to his stall one day and said, "Hey, you! I bought some fish off you yesterday and it were rotten." He said, "Ee, did you? When did you buy it?" She said, "I bought it on Wednesday." And he said, "Ee dear. Tha should have bought it on Tuesday, it were all reet then."'

When people did die, by committing suicide, victims of the poverty and despair which stalked the Lancashire milltowns in the first half of this century, it was often John Parkinson who first came across them. He worked for the Manchester collieries on the canals and his boat became known as the Bodysnatcher. It was built in such a way that if there was a body in the water, the rudder always picked it up and it got caught around the propeller. Such incidents had to be reported to the coroner and there was a fee to compensate the canal man for loss of earnings for having to attend the coroner's inquest. But different areas paid different rates. Some paid five shillings, others ten. When John Parkinson objected to the Worsley coroner at only being paid 5 shillings for finding a body, the coroner gave him a dressing down. "You are nothing but a veritable Burke and Hare of the maritime tradition, Parkinson," he was told. "There's no way we're paying you any more." After that when people saw John coming they'd say, "Here he comes, Billy Burke, the Edinburgh bodysnatcher."'

In Burnley, canal suicides often took place close to the mills, according to the observations of policeman Lynn Millard. The water was slightly warmer near a mill after it had been returned from the condensers in the mill boilers.

'We had a lot of suicides, mainly gassings. Gassings, hangings and throat cuttings with a cut-throat razor,' says Lynn. 'Hangings were from the banisters of stairs, where it was convenient to hang a rope and jump off. They often suffocated rather than broke their necks. But in those days, I don't think the pathologists were right fussy about the cause of death unless there were suspicious circumstances.'

There's a certain callousness creeps into some of these descriptions of death. Maybe it's because times have changed so much that they seem distant days and different people, not our own flesh and blood ancestors. And in those days death was more commonplace as more people succumbed to illness and life expectancy was shorter. With bodies laid out in front rooms for visitors to inspect or standing in their coffins presiding over their own wakes, like Alice Nutter's Granddad Flynn, death was more in the open and held less terror. It's certainly quite extraordinary to us now to learn that Mary Cockle and her friends when they were children would knock on a door and ask to see a dead neighbour:

'We used to come home from school, and if any of our neighbours had died we used to go and knock at the door and say, "Can we look at Mrs Leonard, or whoever it was." That's what they did in those days. We made it our business to have a look at them, and it brought you up to face death.'

Today's over-reliance on drugs and medicines has brought its backlash. I've not heard of a return to hanging boiled potatoes round your child's neck or drinking soot, but there has been a revival in the use of herbal and natural medicines. Val Thome of Nelson doesn't trust modern doctors:

'We grew up in my generation in the 1950s to treat doctors like gods who knew everything and would cure everything. But then from experience, you see what they are doing to people. That everything they give you destroys some other part of your system, and they'll admit this if you ask them. You can't dispense with doctors for their power of diagnosis. All I want the doctor for is to identify the problem then I'll deal with it myself, not by their drugs but by herbal and natural medicines. They've been around for thousands of years and have always worked. And if they don't cure you, they're not going to harm you.'

So perhaps Lizzie Hartley's father's pills deserved their reputation 85 years ago. Though if you visited him then for anything else, you might be advised to take Lizzie's account of what happened with a pinch of salt:

'Now then. When I was at home, a lady came one night, and they called my father Joe. And she said, "Ee, Joe, I had to come. I'm eating and eating, and I'm going thinner and thinner." He said, "Yes, you will." She said, "Can you cure me?" "I'll cure you," he said. "Start today," – it was Monday – "From now till Friday, don't have nothing in your mouth, not a morsel of anything. And come and see me again on Friday." Well, she came and she was very thin. He went into the kitchen and he got a piece of bread and he buttered it. And he came to her and he just put it to her mouth. And out it came! And it was a tapeworm, and it went twice round our backyard. And it had been eating everything that had gone into her mouth. She never had another.'

Chapter Fifteen

Beliefs and Fears

O<small>N THE DAY</small> they buried Alice Whittle's mother in Farrington church cemetery, she was convinced she could hear her knocking.

'When we came back to the house for sandwiches for the relatives, I thought, "What have they put my mum there for?" And I got my bike down from the side of the house and went to Farrington church. And I thought I could hear her knocking. I thought I could hear my mum knocking! And I couldn't pedal fast enough. And I'm thinking, "She's not dead. What have they put her down there for? She's not dead." I slung my bike on the floor and went to her. And the first thing I saw was this mound of flowers. And I stood there, my eyes were streaming and I called, "Mam! Mam!" And then, all at once there was this silence, a deathly silence in the churchyard. And I remember thinking. "My mum's there and I won't see her any more."'

Central to people's system of beliefs is the notion of what happens to them after death. And, to judge from the people I've spoken to, here in Lancashire we're as forthright in this matter as we are in everything else. A blunt and uncompromising life in the mill, where you either knuckled under and worked or you starved. A climate and environment as hard-edged as the rocky outcrops that police our valley sides. It doesn't breed waverers. So I didn't meet many don't knows when it came to religion. It was either an unflinching conviction that Heaven awaited them or an equally courageous ability to stare into the abyss and declare: There's nothing out there. Nothing at all.

Emma Edge belongs firmly to the everlasting life camp. It's something you can't fail to notice when you meet the really old: they might look frail and keep their beds downstairs, but there's a steely determination required to see you through a hundred years on this earth. And when the body fails, the will can continue to propel them on. Emma'[s religious convictions belong to the same steel reinforcement kind. She was converted in 1918 and was preaching at chapel until she was 90. So when her husband Fred died, there were no doubts or despair in her mind:

Ranks of
tombstones,
Haggate Baptist
Church, near
Burnley.

'When Fred died he were in t' front room. And just as they are putting
the first screw in the coffin, I was sat at t' side of the coffin and God said
to me, "Thine be the glory. Risen, conquering Son." And it's 20-odd years
since and I'll never forget it. And do you know, I could have danced in
that front room. And somebody said to me after, "Ee, you did do well,
you never shed a tear." I couldn't have shed a tear for the life in me,
because Christ was there.'

At 95, George Howarth has just as firm a hold on life today as he had
on that steer he wrestled in a rodeo in Nelson when he was a lad. So it
comes as no surprise that he never gives the idea of death or the afterlife
a second thought. When pressed, however, he told me:

'I'd be happy enough if there were a bowling green up there. Do you
think there will be? Or a snooker table? If there's a club up there, I'll join.'

And then, as befits a no-nonsense butcher who has spent a lifetime
sticking pigs and filleting steaks, he adds, 'No, I'll tell you what I think
happens to you. It's like looking at that tree out there. At t' back end,
when those leaves fall, they disintegrate, they just fade away. And that's
what happens to you, you waste away to nothing. If you could get out of

that coffin, you would just blow away in the wind. When you've finished, you've finished. There's no doubt about it.'

When Alice Whittle lost her husband at an early age, she could find nothing for her comfort:

'When Norman died so suddenly, my faith went to pot. The only question I could ask was Why? Why has the Lord done this to me? I was brought up as a Methodist and looked forward to going to chapel. My dad used to say, "Our Alice is the only one that has a bit of faith in her." But when Norman died it went to pot. And I remember, it would be a couple of weeks after Norman died, a knock came to the door. And it was this lady, and she had about four roses, and she said, "I go to the United Reformed Church and we heard about your sad loss. Will you accept these from me?" So I invited her in and put the kettle on and we had a cup of tea. And she asked me if I had any faith. I said, "I did until this happened over Norman. I'm left with a little lad at my time of life, 49 years old, no wage, no nothing. I keep asking the good Lord why, but there's no answer." And she said, "Will you do something for me before I go? The next time you say your prayers, will you not ask the good Lord why, will you give him thanks for the strength He's given you to carry on." And that was the turning point for me.'

A strong tradition of religious non-conformity has always existed in Lancashire, but industrialisation and scientific advance have exposed an underlying vein of scepticism, particularly amongst the men. From Albert Morris's early years collecting and classifying wild fruits and grasses, to his love of beekeeping, building early radio sets and an incurable curiosity to know how things work which finds him undaunted by modern technology, even at 77, has developed an outlook of scientific rationalism. And this is the position he takes on religion:

'It doesn't make sense. It was in the local paper recently, a woman goes to church and on the way out she gets knocked down and killed. To me, this so-called loving God would be the biggest tyrant you could think of it he would allow all this to happen; all the floods and wars and disasters. Can you tell me what parent could stop himself interfering if their child was going to be hurt or anything? No matter how much they tried to let that child have free will, they would interfere.'

Titus Thornber is in the same mold as Albert Morris. History, archaeology, geology, engineering, he's an old-fashioned polymath. When he speaks, you listen to an authority, a man who can draw on knowledge from a dozen different quarters; an endlessly refreshing and resourceful mind. We stand in his barn, and one moment he's pointing out the holes in the beams where the Saxon timbers once fitted, the next he's discussing the peculiarities of the engine of an old Jowett car. You might expect his thoughts on human immortality to be as sharp-edged as his mind still is at 88:

'I think it's supreme arrogance on the part of man to think that he is any better than any other animal. We're only animals, just like those sheep in the fields. We don't talk of an afterlife for them. Why should there be one for us? Man has become so arrogant. He thought he was so much better than the beasts of the field, therefore he must be so wonderful he can never die. But you do die. And that's the end of you.'

Another thing that Albert Morris and Titus Thornber have in common is that both decided they were atheists while at school and they've found no reason to change their minds since. It must have taken quite a lot of courage to come to such a decision in those days. I remember when I was a lad, a lot more recently, we had a neighbour who was a professed atheist and member of the Communist party. He was looked on with nothing short of scandal by the God-fearing and respectable citizens of Colne. Such was the power of church and chapel in milltown communities until into the 1950s, that atheists were virtually demonised.

'The word atheist is still regarded by many with shock and horror,' says Lynn Millard, a humanist. 'I think people have pictures of drunken, raving, violent people who are completely out of control.' Lynn's mentor was a man called Jack Clayton who was a silk weaver in Nelson. 'There used to be a speakers' corner on the steps of Burnley Market where evangelists and political parties used to have their say in the 1950s and Jack used to speak on atheism. He was a self-taught man but a fearsome debater. But they were views which in those days could turn you into a social outcast and you may even have lost your job.'

When we are extolling the virtues of tight-knit communities like we had in Lancashire in the early years of the century and before, of how we helped one another out in times of hardship and shared a strong sense of belonging, it is easy to forget the powerful pressures placed on individuals to conform. I imagine many a Jude the Obscure, sitting in his damp work clothes at WEA lectures in the Mechanics' Institute, being stirred by intellectual flames his workmates, neighbours and family might never share. Then our milltown valleys might seem a cold and sunless climate, and hopes and dreams of intellectual enlightenment might wither on the branch and end in loneliness and frustration.

Today, Lynn Millard conducts special humanist funeral ceremonies for non-believers. What are his own beliefs?

Val Thome dons some of her pagan regalia in the front garden.

'I don't lead a life being a good citizen in the hope of eternal reward or the fear of eternal damnation. I do it because I believe it's my duty. I think it's the proper thing to do. I believe you come on this earth, you do as much good as you can, you enjoy it, and when you die that's it, full stop. End of story.'

Lynn Millard has an unlikely ally in his scorn for the notion of eternal damnation in the Reverend Ian Robbins.

'I have a horrible memory of a head-teacher in a Church of England school marching onto the stage in assembly and saying, 'Hands together, close your eyes, bow your heads and say after me, "O God, we have been very naughty today." Appalling. What parent would begin their encounter with their child by saying, "You've been a bad lad?" The Church in the past has been constantly negative about sex and about human nature. But there is a positive tradition which says we are fundamentally good. We may go wrong because we've got freedom, we may make mistakes and there are mistakes in Creation, awful things that we don't understand that give us germs and diseases and God knows what, but the whole Creation must be fundamentally good and human nature is potentially good. And this belief goes right back to the Celtic tradition which saw God at work in everything they were doing from lighting the fire to milking the cow. So He's there today in everything in life: there in sex, there in money, and that's the way I want to see it.'

Val Thome is a pagan and her religion of Wicca dates back to Celtic times. She believes in many gods in Nature.

'Because not many people are into this religion, these gods have a lot of time on their hands, so you don't have to wait in a queue like with your Christian God who hasn't got a lot of time because people are always berating Him for all these famines and things. So our gods are just sitting around reading the *Nelson Leader* – it's hard to know when Val's being serious, but that's her charm – 'waiting for people to ask them to do something!'

Recently, when Val went on holiday she went round putting her gods in charge of different plots in her garden. 'They're helpful gods. They don't

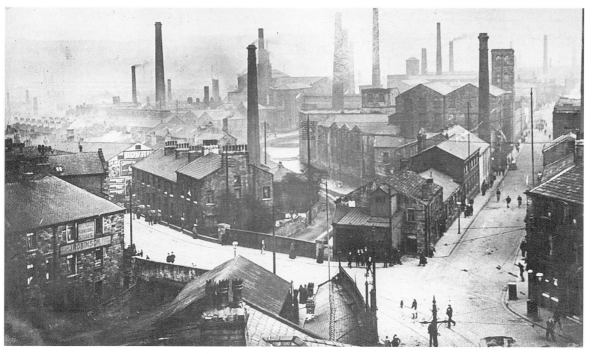

The doctrine of deferred gratification promised a better life in the hereafter than the present. Westgate, Burnley, described by Titus Thornber as a 'hell hole'.

need placating like your vengeful Christian God. What sort of an attitude is it to be seen by your religion as an unworthy sinner? Or always getting it wrong? Plus the attitude, men are in charge? Men are in charge and women are evil, aren't they, in the Christian religion? I'm not having that about wives having to obey their husbands, either, and the man is the head of everything. Well, sorry, mate. I used to go to church and sing "She" all the time, when they were talking about God. In a very loud voice.'

I wonder how a follower of Wicca – a witch to you and me – would have been treated 50 years ago? We have a rather poor record of tolerance in Lancashire if you care to go back even further.

Another person without much time for organised religion is Stanley Graham. As a former engine tenter in the mill and a shrewd scholar of the Industrial Revolution, he has some interesting insights into how organised religion kept our milltown ancestors on the straight and narrow:

'The doctrine of deferred gratification is something which was invented by the Church and the people who started the Industrial Revolution. It preached that it doesn't matter how rough things get in this life, if you keep your nose to the grindstone, your shoulder to the wheel and leave no stone unturned, in the next world you will have a better life. The only problem about that is that nobody has ever come back to tell us that it is actually so.'

Betty Moore thinks that her late mum is sometimes with her. 'The day she died, on that evening I slept in a bed-chair with her, and all of a sudden in the middle of the night, I could feel a hand clasp my hand and I opened my eyes and there she was. She had a fuzzy white thing around her face but she was smiling at me.'

And Cath Howley devoutly believes that her deceased relatives are still with her, especially her father:

'I know that he's wherever I want him to be. Wherever I am that day and I need to talk to him, he's there. There's a presence. And not just my father but my grandparents. My mum's mum was a great influence on my life. She was plagued with a lovely vagueness. I'd take her out shopping and I'd lose her. Or we'd go shopping and she'd try three suits on and I'd say, "Which one do you want, nanna?" And she'd say, "I don't know. I think I'll have them all." And whenever I do anything silly, I know she's there and laughing.'

Val Thome believes that as you get older you lose your fear of death. 'It becomes more friendly. And when people you have known start to pass over to the other side, there'll be more and more people there, waiting for you. So in the end it would seem unkind not to join them.'

'Since coming to the old religion, death is very much a natural part of life. Like the natural progression of the seasons, everything grows and has its life and goes back to the earth. And we're part of that. And being aware of another spirit side of life existing alongside this one, I don't think that anyone I know has gone very far. I really think it's like stepping through a door. My son once sent me a card, and it has a woman in a greenhouse, or more like an indoor conservatory, and at the back there's a door and that leads through into another greenhouse beyond the glass. And I think death is just like that: stepping through that door in a glass wall and when you get there you can still see everything that's going on here. The moment of dying must be like that: like going through a very dark door.'

The Reverend Ian Robbins is not dismissive of spiritualism:

'There's much more to life than what we in a very materialistic world take account of. A scientist was saying on the radio only today: 'The mind is much more than the brain and the soul is that which survives the death of the brain.' And as far as believing in our own resurrection and the continued existence of all those numberless people who have already lived on the planet, the Reverend Robbins says:

'I mean, if you were to have said to someone 50 or 100 years ago, I will show you a machine that has umpteen megabytes and can keep and record all these items of knowledge, he would have said, "I don't believe it". In other words, what we believe or what we imagine is only a measure of the capacity of our own mind, and the last three or four hundred years have taught us that there is immeasurably more in the Universe than we could conceive with our own little minds.'

But for Emma Edge at 101, it is all a matter of simple faith:

'When I get to bed at night, now I'll say, "God, I'll leave misself with thee while morning." And I thanks God every day for my eyesight, my faculties, my health and strength to look after misself. And there's nobody nobbut God can do it. If I hadn't God, I wouldn't want to live.'

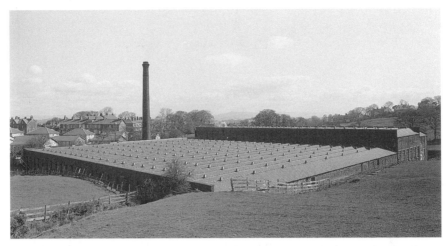

All changed. In five years Bancroft Mill in Barnoldswick had closed and been demolished, and a new housing estate had been built. (*Photos: Daniel Meadows*)

Chapter Sixteen

What's Next?

*W*HEN Emma Edge delivers her verdict on the twentieth century, we'd do well to listen. Born in 1898, she's seen it all: from the terrible harvest of youth in the First World War, to the threat of invasion from Hitler in the Second and the Cold War nightmare of the Bomb. She has lived through the loss of an Empire and the disappearance of a textile industry which in 1913 wove enough cotton to satisfy the home market before breakfast. She has lived through a time of child-labour and shocking slums to one of designer clothes and executive homes, from sheep's head broth to Big Macs, from games round lampposts to drug needles in the park, from herbal cures to antibiotics, from horse and cart to space shuttle, from front doors left wide open to security cameras, from Whit Walks to satellite TV, from Blackpool to Benidorm, from puritanism to the permissive society. No list can accommodate all the astonishing changes of the twentieth century, all of which Emma has witnessed:

'Na then, there's a lot of progress in some things. Folks don't have to start work at 6 o'clock in the morning and they don't have to work as hard. And they get a lot more money. Mind you, they make a bigger fuss of money than what they did in them days. And everybody were poor in them days but they all seemed to cling together more. And their happiness were going in one another's houses and talking, while today they have t' telly on and haven't time to talk. And a lot of 'em thinks about nowt but money these days, and I says, no matter how much they accumulate, they'll not tek it wi 'em.'

It's a widespread feeling amongst the old that today's young people are not as happy as they were. In the past they were poor but happy, and so they question the whole foundation of modern materialism and the belief that money must mean happiness.

'They expect too much these days,' says Ethel Howarth. 'When we were young, the only thing you didn't have was money. But you had a loving family round you; your aunties and uncles were around you because everyone lived near one another. And neighbours looked out for you.'

The drudgery of mill work made to look almost romantic in this study of a cotton mill.

A weaving shed around 1887, looking uncharacteristically spruce. Compare the photograph on page 177.

Colin Waite was a young Mayor of Pendle when I spoke to him (it's not just policemen that get younger), but he nevertheless recognised the importance of a sense of community to our future happiness. His own upbringing on the streets of Padiham during the 1960s is still fresh in his mind:

'The mill reflected the streets: the streets were narrow, you worked alongside each other either at the mill or at the factory, you lived next door to each other. That developed the community spirit. I'm hoping the next generation can recapture some of that togetherness.'

The strong sense of community kept people from straying off the straight and narrow in the past. Old people like Ethel Howarth see today's soaring crime rate and lay the blame at the door of community breakdown:

'If you were doing something you shouldn't have been doing, a neighbour would give you a slap. You went home and told your mother and she gave you another slap for doing it. So you grew up knowing these were things that you hadn't to do because it wasn't right. Whereas now they think that they can do anything they like. Everything is permissible, they seem to think. I mean, look at all this drug-taking. I think the biggest part of the crime is all through this drug-taking because they have to get the money from somewhere.'

Audrey Thornton is deeply pessimistic about the drug problem. Audrey moved from Belfast to live on the Trafalgar Flats in Burnley when they were first built – Burnley's only venture into the ill-fated high-rise living experiments of the 1960s and 1970s. She witnessed the gradual disintegration of the community and the emergence of the teenage problems of the 1980s. But as a social worker, she's seen nothing like the drug epidemic that has spread through the town today:

'It's getting bigger and bigger. Whole neighbourhoods are being destroyed by it. Burnley Wood used to be a lovely neighbourhood to live in, but now it's devastated, devastated. I don't think anyone has an answer. It's no good saying, if the young person had a job, because there are young people who are in good jobs who are still drug addicts. So I don't know what the answer is. I know we haven't hit anything like this before. It's just on the increase. More and more and more.'

Dissatisfaction, an appetite for more and more, fuelled by the consumer society, is seen as the root cause of modern unhappiness by the older end:

'They never have enough,' says Ethel Howarth. 'They want a car and they get a car. Then they want a better car. And then they want a video, and if they can't get one they'll steal one from somewhere. I don't think they're happy. We were happy with the things that were around you.'

Images from the past flood back. Donald Barker meditating beside a crystal pool in the clough above the valley, watching the trout and the water voles. Edgar Wormwell watching six-inch dragonflies and Jenny Whitethroat bobbing into the stream to feed her young in the nest beneath the tree roots. A lost idyll, grown more idyllic perhaps through the rose-tinted spectacles of age and nostalgia, but rendered more innocent by the long fall from grace into our crass and grasping modern culture.

Ron Carter, who could fashion exquisite miniature leaves from dull iron, saw the key to the future in the education of the senses, the reawakening of a sense of wonder in the Universe around us:

'Teach people to observe, their brains and their eyes should be busy. Observation. Wonderful. If a kid had nothing else, he'd be right, like I was without education. I'm just sorry people are deprived, not seeing things. To see the leaves. A leaf is wonderful. It's gobbling up sunshine and it will turn itself towards the sun. The leaf is the mouth of the tree. It's fascinating, isn't it? Everything! And that's only a leaf. We're only touching the edge of it, aren't we?'

But the warning bell is tolling, the bell for the death of nature. Today, when you talk to people, there's almost universal concern for the planet. But we do nothing about it.

'We're poisoning the earth as fast as we can,' says Albert Morris, 'with cars and fumes and various chemicals. I think I've lived through about the best time possible. Between the 1920s and the Second World War as children we've lived in the best of times. I know people will say their parents were unemployed and they had a thin time of it, but all my family and friends agree that the 20s and the 30s were about the best time to live. And then the 40s weren't so bad after the war. But in the 50s things started to go down. I don't think humanity on the earth is going to have a long future unless they find some way of sorting it all out.'

Of course, the end of a millennium is a time for wailing and gnashing of teeth, of forecasts of Doom and Apocalypse, and the people I spoke to didn't let me down. Diane Rogers, who is young and in her thirties and can't be accused of the jaundice of age, is pessimistic, even scared:

'I don't think it can go on much longer. I don't mean next year, but another hundred years of what we're doing. We've meddled with Nature too much. And we're ignoring all the warnings of people like Friends of the Earth and Greenpeace. If you listen, you'd be a bit scared.'

Her sister, Kath Thompson, agrees. 'I don't think the earth is going to explode or there'll be some great catastrophe, but what's going to happen is the world will get hotter and hotter, the ice caps will melt and we'll be completely flooded.' And Kath is prepared to acknowledge her own generation's part in this:

'The responsibility is ours, but because it's probably not going to take place in our lifetime we're not taking it as seriously as we should. But if I suddenly turn green and only use recycled products and do all the things you're supposed to do, it doesn't make any difference. What possible difference can one person make? It's either all or nothing. I think this is how people think. So we go on selfishly using our aerosols, keeping our fridges on, eating our genetically modified foods and so on.'

Angela Arnold is a mother with a young family who believes that technology is moving too fast. 'We don't seem to be able to keep up with it. We know which button to press, but what is it doing to our lives? Apart from making us sit on our fat backsides for even longer. And yet we're still stressed out. How did our forebears manage when they had baking days and washed with mangles and had 18 children and walked to the shops

A Colne street scene today: not much obvious evidence of change here.

but still had time to talk to their friends? How did they find time without all this technology? Did they only sleep for half-an-hour a night?'

Roy Asworth feels so strongly that the world has taken a wrong direction that he has turned his back on it. He's 62 and when I met him he was waiting for the weather to improve then he was off tramping in the Yorkshire Dales with his back-pack and tent, living wild.

'It's as if I reject the present in favour of the past. I don't like the present. I don't like the sophisticated life and I don't know where we're all heading. We can't go on like this. Where's this acceleration in technology going to end? It's become the master not the servant. I've met a lot of people in the last few years and I've spoken to a lot of people in my age group, and there's not one of them said they'd like to be young again today. Now when I was a child my father and my grandparents were envying me the times I lived in. But our generation doesn't envy young people today.'

But the lurking technological nightmares simmer to the surface in the conversation of the organic food specialist and restaurateur, Chris Johnson:

Abandoned looms.

'I attended a conference recently entitled "Transgenic foods and molecular farming". And this is where we come to the agenda of the huge industrial farming which takes place in the United States. And they really don't care if they feed growth promoters to beef animals or grow genetically modified soya or maize, providing that it grows more quickly, grows more cheaply, has a longer shelf-life and at the end of the day makes even more profit for the multi-national companies that produce it. Someone has already developed a chicken where the wings have developed claws, so that one day they'll produce a chicken with four drumsticks. And experiments have taken place putting white chicken feather genes into cauliflowers to make them whiter. It's frightening.'

Stanley Graham thinks that in the next millennium people will come to their senses as far as the money markets are concerned. 'They'll begin to see that rampant capitalism and market forces are not the way forward. That the system we have for managing the world's finances is unstable because of greed and arrogance and some people trying to make too much money for doing very little work.'

The end of a textile empire.

And if Stanley ever goes into politics he has a real vote-catcher when he says, 'Let's run the commanding heights of our economy and our society in the way that best benefits the people of that society. In other words, you don't run a water company to provide the maximum profits for the shareholders. You run it to provide the cleanest, purest, cheapest water to the customers.'

Having survived for five weeks without any money and eating soggy cream-crackers, Diane Colton can't afford to be quite so Utopian in her view of the new millennium:

'There'll still be wheelings and dealings in the House of Commons and people will be getting back-handers. The rich will definitely get richer and the poor will stay as they are.'

As Jim Cropper watches the world whizz past from his farm on Deerplay Moor, surrounded by his sheep and the unchanging hills, he dreams of returning to the days of the horse and cart:

'Everything seems to be going too damned fast for me. When my sheep get out onto this moortop road they get killed instantly because drivers are so impatient. When you're trying to get across the road with your sheep they'll try to knock you and your dog over. There's no patience or courtesy left in this world. Everything's too fast now.'

And an image flashes across the mind of Ben Barnes chugging up Shap in his ancient lorry, a brick on the accelerator as he wees out of the cab door. But it's soon jostled out of the way by a scene of rows and rows of monotonous terraces, smothered in a blanket of soot spewed from a thousand factory chimneys.

'My God, we've gone through some damned awful times,' says historian Ken Spencer. 'The exploitation of working people, class persecution, religious persecution – there's been some horrendous periods in the past and I can't see us ever going back to anything as bad as that again.'

'Every generation has had its shadows of one description or another,' agrees Roger Frost, another historian. 'And we've got different shadows facing us in the new millennium: the shadow of the Bomb, of environmental disaster, all sorts of shadows. But I'd like to think I'm optimistic and that in the future, man will have the ingenuity to overcome any problems which confront him.'